The 21st Century Orator

A complete program to achieve excellence in the public speaking situation

Gil Puga, Jr.

A Local Source Textbook™ Company

Revised: December 2014

The 21st Century Orator

Table of Contents

About Your Instructor

As an instructor I'm constantly giving speeches, I've done nearly 2000 speeches to various student audiences. This may sound extensive, but you'll find that you too will accumulate numerous speeches throughout your life.

I've hosted public speaking events, engineering speeches, educational speeches in other countries, eulogies, and commemorative speaking events.

My research in graduate school was focused on humor appreciation with different source and target factors. Studying speech is a passion of mine, but practicing speech has been my bread and butter money maker. I was on my college forensics speech and debate team. I did Stand Up comedy and children's comedy speeches to pay my way through undergraduate and graduate schools.

After graduate school, I began directing the forensics speech and debate team at Rio Hondo College. I discovered how much I loved speech writing, and putting a speech to the test in a competition. Handing the torch to the young student scholars by showing them how to craft amazing speeches was incredibly gratifying. I coached the team to four national sweepstakes awards, and a state silver award. I'm still in touch with those alumni who I've personally seen go on to excel with that one undeniably vital talent called public speaking. I've given speeches in Universities in Japan and London. I've trained speakers in China and Ireland. And, I've delivered less academic speeches, albeit probably the most important at eulogies for family members and most profound speech coach of all—my mom. I have to say, I love public speaking in all its rich nuances!

It is going to be a complete pleasure to introduce you to the world of public speaking. Over the course of time, you'll do many speeches, each with unique situations. You have a unique perspective and unique expertise that will flourish. It's through effective public speaking that you will be able to *share* that perspective and expertise with others. That's where I come in. I'll work hard to help you develop amazing speech making abilities and treasure each instance that you have the opportunity to speak.

You will find many opportunities to give speeches. Wherever you are, whatever you do: a speech is probably needed to inform, to motive, to commemorate, or even for the simple pleasure of entertaining. So whether it's motivating people to work on pursuing a course of action, or to simply tell a loved one how much you care for them, maybe even a marriage proposal. You will need to do speeches in interviews and meetings. You will need to also be a great listener to sort out the main issues and ask critical questions.

This course is a beginning to building your public speaking knowledge and sharpening your public speaking skills. It is a rehearsal space for your participation in the world. You are going to do many speeches, and this is the beginning.

"Make your speeches powerful, 'wow' your audience and inspire them."

Gilbert Puga, Jr.

About the 21ˢᵗ Century Orator

The *21st Century Orator* (the textbook) is a compilation of theory and activities. It's not designed to the public speaking student an excellent communicator. The *21st Century Orator* is designed as a program for the student to become an excellent speaker across various types of speech situations. My goal is for the student to be able to analyze the speaking context and communicate in an expert like fashion. It could be in a formal speech, a meeting, an interview, a computer enhanced speech, a commemorative or humorous speech. A speech that requires quality proof, otherwise known as evidence. Whatever the situation, a public speaking student who completes this course will conclude with an excitement for future speeches, and the skills and knowledge to really 'wow' his or her audience.

The *21st Century Orator* includes lecture materials written in various forms, typically in an outlined type form, but sometimes as a fill in the blank type form (such as in the Listening section). The *21st Century Orator* is not bound by tradition, rather it is an original compilation to make the student an "excellent speaker."

The *21st Century Orator* includes actual speech assignments and grading sheets for those particular types of assignments, it is in many ways a living text, that is: sections are continuously being added and commented on.

I truly hope you garner the best speech education through *21st Century Orator*. It is a complete guide to achieving excellence in the public speaking situation.

Public Speaking Development Survey (PSDS-1)

Self-Assessment Survey Part 1

Competence Survey: This survey examines your level of speech anxiety, speech preparation ability, outlining, delivery, evidence use, reasoning, and narrative/story use, visual aids coordination, listening, and overall public speaking ability. Answer based on your own assessment of your speaking abilities. For each question, circle only one answer. This survey is not graded based on answers only based on completion.

A. Excitement has to do with the positive emotional anticipation of doing a speech. It is the anticipation of something really positive that is about to occur. How much excitement do you have when you are about to deliver a speech?

1. None
2. Below average
3. Average
4. Above average
5. A high amount

B. If you decided to do a speech in two weeks, which of the below items best resembles how you would prepare for that speech?

1. I would avoid preparing, since I'm good at just speaking off the cuff.

2. I would start by thinking of my speech, although it's unlikely I would have time to write it or outline it, I do like to mentally know what I'm going to say.

3. I would start by writing my speech out, starting with the beginning and going all the way to the end. After everything is written out, I would practice by reading it aloud.

4. I would prepare a lot. My preparation would include speaking and writing. I would start by creating my main points, by saying them and even outlining them. I would think of specific stories and good well-reasoned points. I would also do thorough research; then I would revise and refine the speech. I would then go through my introduction and conclusion in the same manner.

C. Outlining a speech has to do with the ability to highlight the main points of a given speech. This involves grouping the speech into sections, such as the Introduction, Body, and Conclusion. It also involves a visual representation of the speech through enumerations (lettering and numbering the points of a speech). How well can you put an outline together?

1. Not well at all
2. Below average
3. About average
4. Above average
5. I do excellent outlines

D. When presenting a speech, it is often necessary to divide up the speech into various areas/sections in the speech. When you deliver the speech are you able to create distinctive sections with your voice tone and even the wording, such as using transition sentences that help the audience understand clearly the introductory points you are making, each of the main body points you are making, and your concluding remarks?

1. No, this would be very difficult

3. Yes, I can do this

2. Yes, but I would struggle to accomplish this

4. Yes, I'm excellent at this

E. Delivery has to do with your oral presentation of the speech. It involves speaking with eye contact and the effective use of you voice and even body. How well can you deliver a speech?

1. Far below average

4. Above average

2. Below average

5. I have excellent delivery

3. Average

F. When delivering a speech, are you able to state the source (i.e., name of the magazine, date, authors and their credibility, and the basic connection) of your information completely and in less than 45 seconds?

1. No, this would be very difficult

3. Yes, I can do this

2. Yes, but I would struggle to completely and clearly cite the information in that time-frame

4. Yes, I'm excellent at this

G. When delivering a speech, are you able to include specific stories that relate to the point you are making?

1. No, this would be very difficult

3. Yes, I can do this

2. Yes, but I would struggle to give a clear and timely story

4. Yes, I'm excellent at this

H. If you were delivering a persuasive speech where you were attempting to persuade an audience by using good reasoning to support your points, would you be able to do this well?

1. No, this would be very difficult

3. Yes, I can do this

2. Yes, but this would be very difficult

4. Yes, I'm excellent at this

I. If you were to do a speech with visual aids, such as a PowerPoint speech or a Prezi speech; are you able to effectively integrate these computer enhanced visual aids into the speech?

    1. No, this would be very difficult   3. Yes, I can do this

    2. Yes, but this would be very difficult   4. Yes, I'm excellent at this

J. As a listener of Public Speaking, can you make good distinctions between opinion and fact, key issues and minor issues, good reasoning and evidence versus poor or biased reasoning and evidence?

    1. No, this would be very difficult   3. Yes, I can do this

    2. Yes, but this would be very difficult   4. Yes, I'm excellent at this

K. Can you design (write out) and deliver an effective speech?

    1. No, this would be very difficult   3. Yes, I can do this

    2. Yes, but this would be very difficult   4. Yes, I'm excellent at this

Chapter 1: An Introduction to Public Speaking

It was March 2010 in the southern part of Ireland, quite cold that winter. But I was staying in the mystical area of Blarney. The locals would all ask the same question: "Have you kissed the stone? You've gotta kiss the stone." There is a stone on top of the famous Blarney Castle in the city of Blarney which is just north of Cork in Southern Ireland. The Blarney Stone is thought to bestow the mystical powers of speech to anyone who dares kisses the stone. And the famous speaker, Winston Churchill has even stooped down to kiss the stone. So, one breezy sunny day, I climbed up the chambers and corridors to the top of the Blarney Castle. I reached down, got really close, and kissed the Blarney Stone—and according to Irish legend, I should now have the gift of eloquence or based on the local taxi driver from Cork I'd be "able to talk with the ladies much better."

So, does kissing the Blarney Stone give you the powers of speech? We'll answer this question at the end of our investigation into the Nature of Public Speaking?

The Importance of Public Speaking

Public speaking is vital for career development

You need to be an adroit public speaker to attain a job and develop your professionalism. Anyone can be knowledgeable, and that is a noble goal, but to be able to share that knowledge with an audience is even more valuable. Northwest College speech professor, Duane Fish said it best:

> *Regardless of major, regardless of profession or occupation, regardless of experience or expertise, one is, literally, not worth two cents if one cannot express his or her ideas in a manner that can be clearly understood by others. Oral communication is a critical skill for every educated individual.*[1]

There is ample evidence regarding the direct relationship connecting your public speaking ability with your ability to develop and attain a career. Further, if you attain a career and wish to be promoted your public speaking is vital to that goal.

In 1998 a landmark study by the Carnegie Foundation[2] it was found that employers seek graduates who can communicate well. The commissioned study from the Carnegie Foundation for the Advancement of Teaching, highlighted concerns as well. For instance, one concern was the "The failure of research universities seems most serious in conferring degrees upon inarticulate students."

---

[1] D. Fish (personal communication, March 4, 2011). Fish is a speech professor at Northwest College and former
[2] The Carnegie Foundation for the Advancement of Teaching, The Boyer Commission on Educating Undergraduates in the Research University: Reinventing Undergraduate Education (1998). Retrieved from http://naples.cc.sunysb.edu/pres/boyer.nsf/673918d46fbf653e852565ec0056ff3e/d955b61ffddd590a852565 ec005717ae/$FILE/boyer.pdf

Carnegie Foundation Survey - Proportion of Employers who say colleges should place more emphasis than they do today on selected learning outcomes

The ability to effectively communicate orally and in writing	89%
Critical thinking and analytical reasoning skills	81
The ability to apply knowledge and skills to real world settings through internships or other hands on experiences	79
The ability to analyze and solve complex problems	75
The ability to connect choices and actions to ethical decisions	75
Teamwork skills and the ability to collaborate with others in diverse group settings	71
The ability to innovate and be creative	70
Concepts and new developments in science and technology	70
The ability to locate, organize, and evaluate information from multiple sources	68
The ability to understand the global context of situations and decisions	67
Global issues and developments and their implications for the future	65
The ability to work with numbers and understand statistics	63
The role of the United States in the world	57
Cultural diversity in America and other countries	57
Civic knowledge, civic participation, and community engagement	52
Proficiency in a foreign language	45
Democratic institutions and values	40

Public speaking's employment connection is even more apparent when examining all the public speaking occurring in the career context. From the interview, to your ability to share your expertise or motivate others—public speaking is vital to your success.

Public speaking effectiveness is vital for effectively sharing information to an audience: Translation

Have you ever listened to a speech where the speaker took a complex topic and explained it in a way that was totally understandable? Perhaps it's someone explaining a new program or a new technology or even a theory or idea. The skill of communicating a complex idea to lay audience is a hallmark of public speaking called *translation*. Translation is speaking about a technical idea and communicating it in a way that could be understood to even lay audiences. For instance, Dannels studied speech in the engineering field and found that "The most frequent oral communication issue appearing in the Instructional discourse in engineering was the need to translate technical information into a form that was simple and clear for lay audiences."[3]

---

[3] Dannels. D. P. (2005). Communication Across the Curriculum and in the Disciplines: Speaking in Engineering. *Communication Education*

Public Speaking effectiveness is vital to bettering our community

Professor Stephen Lucas notes that "Public Speaking is a vital means of civic engagement" (Lucas, 2012)[4]. In other words, it's important that we communicate our concerns for the betterment of our Community. **Where are some places that you can use public speaking?** Write down as many settings and the potential positive consequences here.

Goals of Public Speaking

There are really three broad areas that are covered in learning Public Speaking as both a speaker and a listener: Cognitive, Behavioral, and Emotion areas. Cognitively, there are many memory aspects. How do you remember your speech best? As an audience member, how do you remember the speaker's speech? Behaviorally, this is the speaker's physical presentation of the speech. You will have to control your nonverbal behavior, or better yet, choreograph your behavior. Emotionally, the speech student should manage his/her anxiety and when you're listening to speeches you still need to control being manipulated by pathos oriented language.

In this course of public speaking you'll increase your public speaking knowledge and skills. You will be introduced to the process of successfully creating speeches. You will increase your knowledge about the speech situation and you'll be able to personalize your speech to meet those strategies. But what constitutes effectiveness for public speaking. When the word effectiveness comes into the picture, another important question arises—effective at what? The answer uncovers some of the key goals for the course. First, there's a cognitive goal, that is the goal of recall. The audience should be able to recall your topic and main points by the end of the speech. In some speech situations you will want your audience to remember even more, perhaps your name (i.e., in an interview) or some key fact or key action that needs to take place. Overall, you should develop your speech with the goal of audience recall.

The second goal is to do a speech where you are viewed as credible. You should be able to develop speeches where you are seen as a trustworthy speaker to the audience, and, you should start to develop a sense of personal credibility. Personal credibility is the self-perception of you feeling that you see yourself as a credible and insightful speaker. If you trust and believe in your message, it's likely the audience will trust and believe in your speech message as well.

An effective public speaker should garner audience recall, establish and maintain credibility, and should move the audience with insightful material.

Goal 1: Speaking in a way where your audience recalls your main points

One of the key goals in learning public speaking is to speak in a way where the audience can recall your intended main points. If you can speak in a way where the audience remembers your main points, you've done a good job. This cognitive function can be difficult but again remember by the end of your speech if your audience can highlight those key points fairly easily then you've done a great job. So, in learning public speaking, you'll need to master the art of organization, delivery, editing to avoid information overload, and all the other public speaking nuances that help the audience come out with a clear understanding of the key points.

---

[4] Lucas, S. (2012). *The Art of Public Speaking.* McGraw Hill, New York, NY

Goal 2: Speaking in a way where your audience believes you, in other words instilling speaking credibility with your audience and yourself

Another goal is to increase your speaker credibility otherwise known as your speaker *ethos*. Credibility is broken down into three key areas: believability/expertise, trustworthiness, and like-ability (Source needed). Think about a college class that you started. The instructors have an advanced degree so you may find yourself listening to the instructor because they have expertise in an area. Then the instructors tell you the following the class they'll bring in a questionnaire for you, and they do. The instructor is trustworthy and believable, hence, you judge the instructor positively. The instructor also communicates in a very friendly manner he smiles and even uses humor well. This general audience judgment stems from the notion of credibility. One goal is to develop speeches where you are seen as that incredibly credible instructor. You'll be able to achieve the like-ability criterion fairly easy with simply treating your audience respectfully and displaying a friendly demeanor. You can also achieve expertise my using evidence in your speech and general appearance, even in your speech delivery. Believability is can also be easily achieved, do what you say, avoid self-deprecating yourself, and keep your speech organized. One major goal is for you to develop a speaker ethos.

To achieve your speaker ethos goals, we'll focus on doing things that increase the audience's favorable rating of you when you start the speech (initial credibility) and as you speak (derived credibility) and at the end of your speech (terminal credibility). Of course it all starts with a speaker's level of confidence to at least give it a go. So, increasing your speaker confidence (Personal ethos) is another related goal. You need to develop enough confidence to be able to speak in public even if it's just being able to ask a simple short question.

Goal 3: Giving outstanding speeches.

Another goal is to help you develop speeches that are personally satisfying and beyond. Sometimes we are our own toughest critics, this means you just have high personal expectations. It also means at the end of the day, the most important audience member is ourselves. Having the ability to (1) develop a speech that adapts to the situation and speeches where you feel good about is important.

Goal 4: Insightful content

A final goal is for you to be able to give insightful speeches. Giving insightful speeches means that you select great topics. It involves narrowing your speech to the best point. Even if your speech is simply a discussion point, your ability to make an insightful point is important. Stephan Lucas captured the importance of going beyond overemphasizing presentation skills

> *In the popular conception, however, it is too often seen chiefly as a matter of spellbinding delivery or of cultivating a winning personality. Leaning to speak clearly and convincingly is a skill—as is learning to write clearly and convincingly—but the most important part of speaking, as of writing, is having something important to say.*[5]

---

[5] Sloan T.O. (Ed.). (2001). *Encyclopedia of Rhetoric.* Oxford University Press. New York, NY.

10

The Origins of Public Speaking

How long have we been doing Public Speaking?

It's difficult to say how long humans have practiced public speaking because humans have probably spoke since their origins. According to Language expert, Jack Fletcher[6] we have been speaking for 4 million years. That date even pre-dates modern humans which goes back to 2.3 to 2.4 million year if the genus Homo, which includes modern humans were used[7]. To contrast public speaking origins, let's compare those origins with the origins of writing.

How long have we been reading, writing, and speaking?

According to Fletcher, we have been writing for 4,000 years. And indeed old Sumerian tablets are evidence for this. In China, the existence of writing on Turtle shells dates back further, perhaps 6,000 years.

What impact does the length of time that we have been speaking have on us?

Humans have been speaking for so long that our neurocircuitry has been impacted. In other words, we have developed the genetics to speak. Two genes that have been identified are the FOXP2 gene and the TOSPEAK gene.

- FOXP2, is one gene responsible for articulate speech. This gene is similar to the other frontostriatal and frontocerebellar circuits that control motor cortex in the performance of movement[8].
- Tospeak gene: Researchers Raymond Clarke of the University of New South Wales' St. George Hospital in Kogarah, Australia, October 21 at the annual meeting of the American Society of Human Genetics. November 21 2009 in Science News[9] discovered the gene, responsible for speech. Dubbed *tospeak*, the gene was found in an Australian family with a speaking disorder.

Because we have been speaking for so long, speaking has become a natural part of us, Fletcher summarizes this

Speech is a biologically evolved skill we have had speech for 4 million years. We have had written language for 4,000 years. We are biologically destined to speak, but not to read or write.

---

[6] Hotz, R.L. (1998, October 18). The Art of Language, the brain matters. *The Los Angeles Times*, p.1.

[7] Wellcome Department of Cognitive Neurology in *Science photo.com.* Brain activity when speaking/listening. http://www.sciencephoto.com/media/307220/enlarge

[8] McHenry, H. M. (2009). Human Evolution. In Ruse, M. & Travis, J. *Evolution: The First Four Billion Years.* Cambridge, MA: The Belknap Press of Harvard University Press. p. 265

[9] Hesman Saey, T. (2009). Gene implicated in speech evolution. *Science News, 176 (11).* p11

Is Public Speaking learned or innate?

Speaking is innate. Unless we have problems with our neurocircuitry, you will speak. Good public speaking is learned. In other words, you're all born with the tools to give "C" level speeches, but if you want to craft the speech to do "A" level speeches, you'll need to learn how to deliver the most effective speeches for given situations. So, Public Speaking is both learned and innate.

Speaker's Corner in London, United Kingdom

Public Speaking Components

Let's start with some of the components of public speaking situation based on early transactional models.

Source is the speaker

Message is the intended meaning of the speech

Content is the words and images (e.g., computer generated images) and objects that are used in the speech

Channel/Medium is the means of a speaker delivering his/her speech to the audience

Receiver is the audience

Noise are the things that interfere with communication

External noise is interference outside of the speaker, such as the sound of a fan or a car or person that interferes with the audience's hearing of the speech

Internal noise is the physiological or psychological interference that distracts audience hearing and listening to the speech message. For instance, psychological noise of worrying about a recent conflict with your significant other can make it difficult to get the speech message. Physiological noise is something inside of us, such as being very sleepy or being sick and so forth.

Encoding is creating the intended speech message

Decoding is deciphering the intended speech message

Design is creating your speech that is the organization and the selected examples and wording, and connectives.

Delivery is the presentation of your speech that is the tone, pace, the physical presentation such as all your nonverbal message that occur during the physical presentation.

Nonverbal Communication: Communication that transcends written communication. For instance, your body movement, tone, pace, gestures

Defining Public Speaking

Public speaking is *the process of a speaker(s) attempting to send an intended communicative message to an audience*

- **Process**: the cognitive, emotional, and behavioral preparation, application, and evaluation of an oral message to an audience
- **Human speaker:** Nonhuman animals communicate as well, but the focus is on human communication
- **Intention:** examining only the speeches that are deliberate Intents
- **Communicative message:** typically this is an oral message or speech act. These are messages that are said and statements that act as a deliberate means of communication
- **An audience:** 2 or more intended listeners. Usually a group of people

Quantitative definition of Public Speaking:

- Intrapersonal (within): This word houses two words within it, "Intra" and "personal." Intra Latin root meaning is "within" or "inside." Personal has to do with persons. Hence, within person, or more exactly intrapersonal communication is communication within oneself or to oneself
- Interpersonal (between): This word houses two root words between, "Inter" and "personal." Inter has a Latin root meaning of "between." Hence, communication between persons, or more specifically, interpersonal communication is communication between two persons
- Public Speaking: is typically a person communicating to a group (audience)

While there are elements of each in public speaking its key to note that there are different expectations for each type. Consider some differences between Public Speaking and Interpersonal Communication:

Distinguishing Public Speaking from Interpersonal Communication (everyday interactions)

Expectation Violation Theory claims that we enter all communicative interactions with expectations. These expectations are based on our values and cultural scripts. Let's apply some general notions to expectations and look at public speaking and interpersonal communication.

Comparing Public Speaking to Interpersonal Communication

Public Speaking expectations	Interpersonal Communication expectations
• More planned (Verbal/NV)	• Less planned: "hidden agenda"
• More Formal	• Less formal: incomplete sentences, cuss words, slang
• Clearly defined roles	• Less role emphasis/equals
• Further proximity	• Closer Proximity
• Longer sustained messages	• Short messages: if they're too long, you been "lectured" to
• More direct eye contact received	• Only one person giving us direct eye contact, and not too long
• If no sound amplification, more vocal projections	• Moderate to low vocal projection

What's the difference between a public speaking and speech?

Public speaking and speech overlap. Both are arguably the same but to understand the distinction try to consider speech as broader than public speaking. To help understand this distinction, consider a speech act or an action that you may take that is indeed a message but the speaker is not verbally saying anything. For instance, if you donate money to a political candidate did you know that that is seen as speech? Your speech act in that instance is "I approve of this candidate" or if you were to go to a city or school council meeting wearing a bright red shirt in support of an issue or person that is considered speech.

In the 1968 Olympic in Mexico City, two US Olympic champion athletes, Tommie Smith and John Carlos walked up to the medal stage along with Australian athlete Peter Norman. The two American athletes were wanting to say something about the poor treatment of African Americans in the US. What do you suppose they should do? How about the Australian athlete?

The nature of speech from an intelligence perspective

In 1982, Howard Gardner's "Frames of Mind" was published[10]. Gardner identified several intelligences. Linguistic intelligence is strongly connected to your speech making ability. This intelligent type is connected to your ability to use language, including your story telling ability.

Are you someone who can keep an audience riveted to a story you're telling? If are or if you know someone who is, it's probable that your seeing linguistic intelligence at play. Consider some of the popular public speaking figures such as Abraham Lincoln or Martin Luther King, Jr. they could tell a great story and likely had a high degree of linguistic intelligence.

Linguistic intelligence is characterized by someone with highly developed oral and written

---

[10] Gardner, H. (1983). *Frames of Mind.* Basic Books: New York: NY

communication skills, knowledge of the many different uses for language; such as persuasion, information, or pleasure. Public speakers, stand-up comedians, poets, and writers are people with linguistic intelligence.

There are many online assessments to see where you are regarding your abilities. Try this website to see where you place: http://literacyworks.org/mi/assessment/findyourstrengths.html.

The Challenge of Meaning

Let's start with the "Communication as Action" model. It essentially posits that a source sends a message through a channel and that message is received by the receiver or the audience. It sounds simple enough but there is one incredibility challenging aspect to this model. Can you find it?

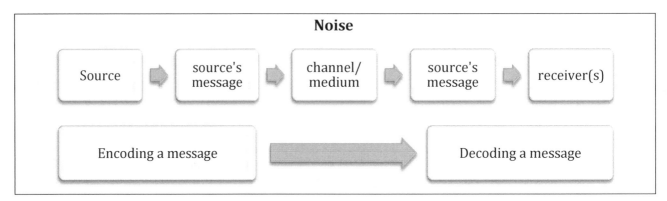

How many meaning variations can you come up with when listening to the following oral message?

Today, while you sit in this classroom at this college, you will learn something that will have a great impact on your life.

Suppose this is the general message that you intend to send. Now say it with varying nonverbals and varying stresses on words. Uh oh, the phrases meaning changes. In fact, we, as the source of the message may even put "filler's" into the sentence or simply misstate the message. The receiver may be not even listening, or if they are listening they may be selectively listening or thinking of something totally different while pretending to be listening. You've likely experienced these scenarios. These scenario speak to the challenge of the receiver actually getting your intended original intended message.

The challenge with linear models of communication, is that meaning is in people. Hence, we need to make sure our intended meaning is on target with what we want to convey. This is the difficulty of encoding (creating) the message or speech that exactly aligns with the meaning we are trying to convey. As for the receiver, this too is very difficult to ensure that the audience (receiver) get your meaning.

Getting the audience to comprehend what you're saying

A Princeton University study found that audience's brain activity in the prefrontal cortex were in sync with the speaker albeit with a short lag of about one second. If the listener, however, fails to comprehend what the speaker is trying to communicate, their brain patterns decouple. In the *Proceedings of the National Academy of Sciences*[11] July 26 2010. This is similar to the idea Emotional Contagion theory. In sum, this theory posits that the audience will be in the same state as the speaker.

As a speaker, for each of your topics, care about them, speak with an intensity of the topic. If you communicate clearly and passionately, your audience will be with you all the way.

Situational nature of Public Speaking

All public speaking is situational. Consider the region, the time, the circumstances, the audience, and so forth. Those situational aspects will surely change by your next speech. In most cases, when you're asked to do a speech, you won't be given specific detailed guidelines like in a formal college level speech course. You will actually need to discover and predict the parameters of the speech. To create parameters consider all the basic questions: How long should I go? Should I use visual aids/computer? Should I use humor? What's the audience's mood? And so forth. The Rhetorical Situation deals with a speeches specific time, place and circumstances. Rhetoric is the use of words and symbols to achieve a goal. Consider how would you ask a friend to lend you money? You probably wouldn't say "I need $20, lend me $20 now." You would change the order and the words and think of the situation. We do those throughout the day. Perhaps you would say "Hi friend, you know you're a great friend. You're not going to believe this, but I forgot my wallet. I have $20 at home, but I really needed it to pay for my book. Can you lend me $20 and I will pay you back next week in class?" Crafting the message to meet your goal is being rhetorical.

Blarney Castle is seen here across the bridge. As the story goes, in 1314 during Robert the Bruce, in spite of being outnumbered defeated of the English army at Bannockburn. It was then that the stone was divided into two, and the King of Munster sent half the stone to Blarney, Ireland. Later a witch who was saved from drowning revealed its mystical power.

---

[11] *Proceedings of the National Academy of Sciences* (2010 July 26). Source cited in Scientific American Mind

Conclusion

As for the Blarney Stone, yes, I kissed it. Hopefully, I now have the gift of gab. But, I will share with you, something that isn't legend but is fact. I've seen it over and over when I was directing the speech team and judging weekend speeches. A student speaker will start out, sometimes awful, actually most times awful. But they will be there at the next tournament, and I would see an improvement. Not great—just better. Then the next tournament they would be there. And I would notice wow, they actually were competitive. Then the next weekend tournament would come and that student would be there. I would notice that the student got into the final rounds. Then the next tournament, they won: 1st place. And at the next tournament, I'd hear people whisper: wow, he's a natural/he just has it. But, I will tell you now, something that is true, you need to work on it to become a great speaker. The great news though, you don't have to travel to Blarney Ireland and kiss a stone to be a great speaker, no my friends, you just need to be fully committed to learning the art of public speaking. And you have to do several speeches to be a great public speaker! Good luck on your voyage!

A Historical Perspective of Public Speaking from 2000-2012

In the early part of the 21st century public speaking began a radical technical transformation. The popularity of computer programs such as Microsoft's PowerPoint enabled speakers to insert visual aids into speeches. Some memorable speeches from 2000-2012 highlight the pervasiveness and influence of visually enhanced computer generated presentations, most notably from the accessible Microsoft program known as PowerPoint.

One significant speech that was given in the wake of attacks on the World Trade Centers in New York and the U.S. Pentagon was from Colin Powell to the United Nations Security Council. This persuasive speech was delivered on February 5, 2003. The speech was aimed at attaining support for the US lead invasion of Iraq. Powell infused visual photographic images as evidence the Iraq had or was very near to attaining Nuclear weapon capability. The speech was persuasive but should also highlight the importance of not taking images at face value. Powell himself came to critique the information that he presented. In the aftermath of the Iraq war, the premise for the invasion was found to be untrue (i.e., Iraq did not have nuclear weapons).

The military often used computer generated images, such as PowerPoint to inform staff. In April 26, 2010, the New York Times highlighted some problems with PowerPoint, namely that the program created the illusion of control and that some problems were "not bullet-sizeable." Perhaps most illuminating in the critique was that PowerPoint "stifled discussion, critical thinking and thoughtful decision-making."

Computer based speeches were also abundant in education. One popular book, *The Last Lecture (2007)*, exemplifies this trend. Author and Computer Science Professor Randy Pausch details his final lecture to his students. Pausch had terminal cancer and hence the lecture was beyond teaching about computer science and more about a call to follow one's childhood ambitions. His lecture was based on slides and the significance of each slide. Pausch's speech highlights that ability of speeches through PowerPoint to be personal. Though during this juncture in academia, PowerPoint was quite typical in the higher education classroom.

Finally, a notable speech was the film *An Inconvenient Truth (2006)*. This film by Al Gore went on to become an Academy Award Best Documentary Feature. The film was centered on informing the public about global warming. The film was included Gore's PowerPoint-like presentations regarding CO^2 levels and other environmental challenges facing the world. Gore went on to become the Nobel Peace Prize winner of 2007. This highly influential film showed that a PowerPoint-like presentation can be influential, persuasive, and credibility enhancing.

Although there are several places where speeches occurred void of computer generated visual aids, such as Steve Job's 2005 Commencement speech at Stanford University or Presidential *State of Union* speeches, clearly computer-generated images for public speaking was the zeitgeist of the times in the first decade of the 21st century.

The History of Public Speaking: From Oratory, to Public Speaking, to Communication

Based on Lucas' historical analysis of public speaking in the *Encyclopedia of Rhetoric* (Sloan, 2001), we can see some unique trends that have occurred. From 2001- current, can you see much more of an impact from technology.

1. In the ancient world, what was the only medium to reach the mass audience?
2. What were public speakers referred to before the 20th century?
3. In the 1920's college elocution and oratory courses were retitled as _____, this emphasized the _____.
4. Around the end of the 19th century, in a departure from the neoclassical model of oratory, _____ citizens of ordinary mean begin to speak. In addition, the oratorical set piece gave way to _____ addresses.
5. During the Great Depression and World War II, Franklin D. Roosevelt gave his most famous group of speeches known as the "fireside chats." These radio delivered Fireside Chats were_____.
6. What allowed "even the most subdued speaker to be heard in almost any setting"?
7. What was the #1 speech according to the Top 100 American Speeches Survey?
8. What is the "single most important mode of expression for people seeking to broaden the lines of power and privilege in American society"?
9. Who suffered from severe stage fright, but went on to become the most universally admired speaker in the 20th century?
10. Who was in spite of being perhaps the most magnetic speaker, the most malevolent speaker in the 20th century and what does this tell us in regard to what should guide the power of the spoken word?
11. Is rhetoric inherently moral or immoral?
12. What is the articles position on "efforts to protect society by restricting free speech"?
13. What's the author's position on public speaking and the major political revolutions during the twentieth century? Do you believe cultural movements such as political revolutions will need to be fueled in substantial measure by the spoken word? Discuss.
14. From 2000-2012 we can examine speeches such as Colin Powell's 2004 speech to the United Nations, Al Gore's speech that became the highlight of his movie, The Inconvenient Truth, and even more personal speeches such as The Last Lecture. What unique characteristics and unique critiques do they warrant?

Chapter 2: Anxiety Management

"If you can't communicate and talk to other people and get across your ideas, you're giving up your potential."

Warren Buffett
Billionaire Philanthropist and Investor
(3rd wealthiest person in the world, 2014)

What does actress Nicole Kidman and scientist Albert Einstein have in common?

Throughout this course you will have opportunities to explore ways that you can manage stress. Please, do "explore." Anxiety management is accomplished, in part, by your own personal experimentation. So, if something works for you--use it! One great thing about this course is that you will be learning public speaking skills. Skill acquisition is in itself a way to manage anxiety. Remember, as assistant professor of communication studies Paul Witt (at Texas Christian University) says: "Virtually every speaker gets nervous most of the time, or at least some of the time."

The science behind Public Speaking anxiety

During state anxiety we experience neurochemical reactions that end up secreting cortisol into the bloodstream.[12] The two primary symptoms of anxiety are (1) conscious rumination (i.e., worrying) and (2) heightened sensitivity to body sensations.[13]

Public Speaking anxiety is managed in part by having a thorough understanding of its underlying foundations. There are several basic research findings going into our investigation of anxiety.

Types of anxiety

There are two types of anxiety. Trait anxiety and state anxiety. Trait anxiety is the anxiety that we generally have. It is a biological construct that deals with our innate response to stress. State anxiety has to do with the situation. Research indicates that Trait anxiety is about 57% of our anxiety. State anxiety is about 20%

Anxiety stages

Public speaking anxiety has been found at several stages, just prior to the speech is the first stage, called the **anticipatory** stage. The next stage occurs when speakers began speaking, this is called the **confrontation stage.** The ending part of the speech is the **adaptation stage.** When the speech is over is the **release stage.** During the anticipatory stage our anxiety (measured through cortisol release) is at its highest levels. There is a significant drop off after the speech progresses.

---

12 Marshall, P.J. & Stevenson-Hinde, J. (2001). Behavioral inhabitation: Physiological correlates. In W.R. Crozier & L.E. Alden (Eds.), *International handbook of social anxiety: concepts, research, and intervention relating to the self and shyness* p.53-76 NY: Wiley & Sons

13 Gray J.A. & McNaughton, N. (2000). *The neuropsychology of anxiety.* Oxford: Oxford University Press

Anxiety and the type of speech

Research has found that the type of speech will impact your anxiety levels. If we examined a speaker's anxiety along a continuum of three types of speeches we would find different amounts of anxiety. If delivering a *manuscript speech*; where the speaking has the word for word speech to read from, (2) *extemporaneous speech*; where the speaker has note cards and has reviewed the broad content, and (3) *impromptu speech*; a speech with limited preparation, we would find different anxiety results. The highest anxiety would be found if the speaker were delivering an impromptu speech. The second highest would be found in the extemporaneous speaking area. The least amount of anxiety compared to the other two speech genres would be found in the manuscript speech area. Three key anxiety management aspects to keep in mind are:

- ☐ Anxiety management is the goal; not eliminating anxiety.

- ☐ Gage your anxiety levels and try to increase or decrease depending on your levels. Most of you will probably need to decrease your anxiety.

- ☐ You can manage your anxiety, but you will need to put effort into learning and trying to manage.

Recent research on Anxiety is that Anxiety levels for public speakers tends to be at its highest levels at the just before the speech and at the very start of the speech. After the speech has commenced, the anxiety levels decrease throughout. For interview type speeches, anxiety tends to be steady throughout. Given these findings, for public speaking the beginning should be very well prepared. For meetings or interviews, try to remain attentive throughout.

Public Speaking Anxiety and Interview Anxiety[14]

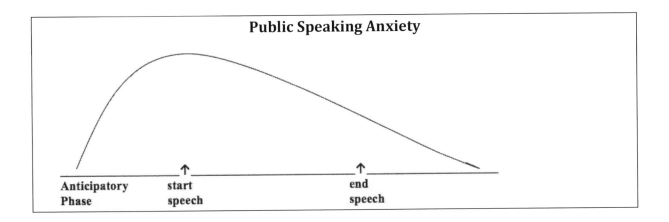

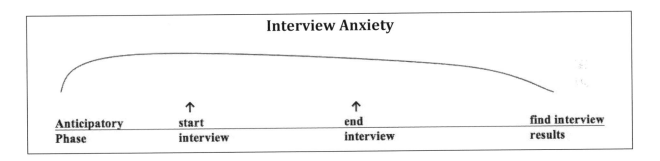

[14] Young, M.J., Behnke. R.R., & Mann, Y. M. (2004). Anxiety patterns in employment interviews. *Communication Reports*. 17 (1), p 49

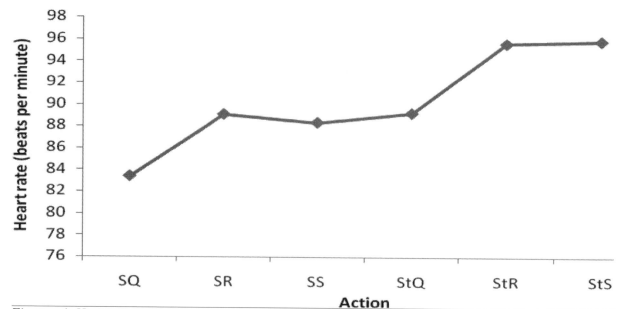

Figure 1 Heart Rate Across Six Experimental Conditions. Note. SQ = Sitting Quietly; SR =Reading While Sitting; SS =Speaking While Sitting; StQ = Standing Quietly; StR = Reading While Standing; StS= Speaking While Standing.

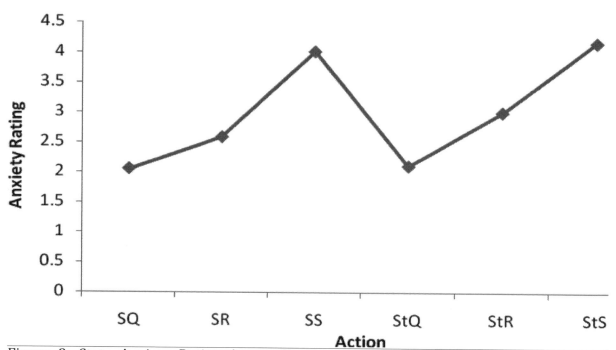

Figure 2: State Anxiety Rating Across Six Experimental Conditions. Note. SQ =Sitting Quietly; SR = Reading While Sitting; SS =Speaking While Sitting; StQ = Standing Quietly; StR = Reading While Standing; StS=Speaking While Standing.

Understanding the causes of Public Speaking anxiety

One way you can reduce public speaking anxiety is to understand its causes. Here are two causes of public speaking anxiety: (1) when one faces a new/different situation. As one becomes more familiar with the speaking situation, he/she becomes desensitized to the anxiety. Hence, doing several speeches over the course of time will lead to a decrease of anxiety (systematic desensitization); (2) conspicuousness (feeling of being watched) or judged.

18 Techniques and Considerations For Managing Anxiety

These techniques and considerations come from my own many public speaking experiences, including my own trial and error methods, and coaching speakers, and from many suggestions from current public speaking books out there, and research findings from peer reviewed studies.

1. **Get started early**

   If you are having difficulty starting, give yourself a small time goal. For example, aim to work on the speech for 10 minutes. Many times that 10 minutes will stretch into a solid hour or more. Remember the only difference between someone who procrastinates and has intense concentration is the task they are doing. If you feel that you are a procrastinator, give yourself 5 minutes to work on your speech—you'll procrastinate and end up spending 20 minutes on your speech.

   Why start early?

   A. This will give you momentum, and confidence.
   B. Early preparation does not include panic anxiety because of the deadline. Later, preparation does include this anxiety. So, early starts give you a greater degree of quality preparation.
   C. Subconsciously your brain will start preparing for the speech—even when you're not deliberately studying. You will have more chances to have creative epiphanies.

2. **Prepare thoroughly**

   Lucas suggests that for every minute of speech; you should prepare for 1 to 2 hours.[15]

3. **Try a rehearsal in front of a mirror**

   If you have particularly high anxiety, mirror-based practicing may help. One study by Smith and Frymier found positive effects from mirror-based practices. The authors suggested that the speaker can monitor his or her nonverbal communication behaviors, such as posture, gestures, etc.).[16]

---

[15] Lucas, S. (2012). *The Art of Public Speaking.* McGraw Hill

[16] Smith, T.E., & Frymier, A.B. (2006). Get 'real': Does practicing speeches before and audience improve performance. *Communication Quarterly, 54(1),* 111-125. doi: 10.1080/01463370500270538

4. Visualize succeeding

This involves viewing a successful speech and visualizing yourself giving a successful speech. Performance visualization reduces anxiety. Performance visualization for a speaker involves watching a videotape of a proficient speaker, making a mental movie of the speaker, and replacing the image of the speaker with a vivid image of oneself as the speaker (Ayer, 2005).

5. Simulate (create) the same conditions during rehearsal as the conditions during the speech

Ideally, to practice a speech in this class with a few people sitting around would be best. But, even at home you can line up a few chairs, imaging that an audience is there, turn off the radio, and time your speech. This run through will help a lot in familiarizing yourself to the actual speech settings.

In one case, one of my former students practiced his final speech in front of his entire family and some relatives in his living room, while they were having a family get-together. Afterward they talked about what they liked and didn't like. The in-class final speech ended up receiving a high score and this speaker went on to receive an "A" in the course.

6. Have someone or a group of people sit and watch you

I have always thought this was the best way to manage your anxiety, and recent research may have confirmed this. A study found that high audience ratings were directly correlated with the rehearsal condition of practicing in front of people.

Speakers who practiced in front of groups of 10 people had the highest ratings when actually performing the speech in front of a live audience. The intermediary ratings came from speakers who rehearsed in front of a small audience prior to the speech. The lowest ratings came from speakers who practiced but never did there speech in front of an audience. Not only does practicing in front of someone help manage anxiety, performance improvements have also been found. In *Communication Quarterly*, communication scholars Smith and Frymier[17] found that speakers who practiced in front of 4 of more audience members had the highest performance ratings compared with practicing in front of 1-3 people or practicing in front of no audience.

So for managing anxiety and increasing your performance level try to at least one person or ideally a group of people to watch your speech prior to actually presenting the final speech.

> Practicing in front of others will enable you to adjust to the unique context of public speaking.

> Don't let your practice-audience interrupt you while you're speaking, unless your speech will involve similar interruptions.

Avoid stopping to talk about the speech. Go through the entire speech, even if you are struggling it's important that you finish everything before you discuss it.

---

[17] Ibid

Day of the Actual Speech

7. Adhere to your usual tendencies

On the day of your anxiety producing event (your speech, test, etc.) adhere to your usual tendencies. When you are really anxious you may do things that are not typical of you out of nervousness.

One expert on anxiety at the University of Northern Colorado says that some people when they are really anxious feel compelled to clean. She said these people would go on a cleaning rampage cleaning their entire room. Try to monitor your behavior; don't do things that are going to interfere with your performance. Adhere to your usual tendencies.

Coffee, cigarettes, alcohol

If you drink a cup of coffee each morning, on the day of your speech you should drink only one cup of coffee as you usually do—don't try to quit; and don't start drinking three cups. The coffee principle is especially important for test taking. The same principle applies to cigarettes. I was once auditioning for a play and before I started I was outside with another student—I was very nervous. She smoked a cigarette and out of my nervous I said "Hey, can I have a cig.?" I don't even smoke cigarettes. Two minutes later I auditioned. During the audition, I not only had to deal with the anxiety but now my body had to deal with the additional challenge of the stuff in the cigarettes (i.e., nicotine). I felt like I was having some sort of out of body experience and worst of all I didn't get the part. I know a lawyer who used to get liquored up before speaking engagements. He claimed that he felt calm but he looked and spoke sloppy. Don't consume alcohol or anything else that will throw your timing off. A study published in *Communication Research Reports* (2007) by University Professors at Northwestern University found a negative relationship with alcohol consumption and speech performance. In other words, increases in alcohol consumption lead to a decrease in speech performance.

Food

Eat as you normally do; but just prior to speech don't eat any food. The last thing you need to worry about is a stomach that is growling. A little bit of water is fine. Some foods can be used as rituals and also have a good utilitarian function these can be powerful and good ways at getting you into the mindset of a good performance. For example, breath mints or lip balm (i.e., ChapStick).

People.

General rule of thumb is limit socializing with people. Because you're anxious you may be more irritable than usual. Try not to manage that big conflict on the day of your speech.

8. Arrive early

There seems to be a direct relationship with waiting-time and anxiety level. The more time you are waiting and thinking about your speech the greater your anxiety will be. If you think you have low anxiety—get there extra early and you will get more pumped up for the speech. Get there 15 minutes early just to run through your ideas and check out the sight. You might want to arrange the speaking area a certain way or at least take a look at the speech setting.

9. Deep breathing

Deep breathing is good as long as it is done with plenty of time to re-adjust to your normal breathing (don't do deep breathing if you are within 5 minutes of your speech). Just prior to your speech you should focus on relaxing your breathing.

10. Stretch out

Tightening muscles then loosening muscles may help. Simple stretches are good tension releasers. Clenching your fist then unclenching your fist.

During the Actual Speech

11. Go with anxiety

Experiment with trying to make yourself more anxious. Increasing anxiety is especially important if you have low anxiety. If you don't have enough anxiety you may appear too cavalier or too informal about the speech.

12. Get excited about the speech

Public Speaking is a great opportunity to tell our story, or share the valuable information you have. Try to frame the anxiety as excitement. Tell yourself "I am excited," rather than "I am calm." A 2013 study found that students who said they were excited rather than calm, had longer speeches that were more persuasive, competent, and they were more relaxed.

13. Before you go up, give yourself a positive statement ("Now I really *wow* them [the audience]")

You worked as much as possible provided the given conditions, now, just go for it. This helps get you into the mindset of performing.

14. Concentrate but avoid being too critical of yourself

Be noncritical during performance. Avoid mumbling any "mistakes"; or that your nervous ("I'm so nervous"). The audience probably doesn't know. Try to avoid correcting word choices during the speech.

15. Consider Flight or Fight response; choose fight

When we panic we have the urge to run away or stand and fight. In terms of a speech, you may feel that things are not going well—hence, you rush through the speech and get off the stage as quickly as possible—this is the flight response to fear. On the other hand, you may feel that things are not going too well; therefore you adjust, you fight through the rough spots by staying committed to your main points increasing your intensity a bit and eventually winning over the audience. This is the fight response.

16. Focus on what you're trying to tell the audience rather than the audiences' evaluation

Focus on describing your main ideas, rather than how the audience feels about you (evaluation) or your main points.

17. Acknowledge and deal with the extremely unusual

If something very unusual happens you may have to acknowledge and deal with it. For example, if your visual aids topple over and fall on the ground—pick the visuals up.

18. Internalize success; externalize failure

Internalizing means attributing (explaining) that something we did was done because of something we are born with (something inside of us).Externalizing means attributing that something we did was done because of something outside of us. For example, a speaker did great on a speech because he or she, is a naturally great speaker (internal). A speaker did poorly because, he or she did not practice enough (external). If you really want to have fun with this concept practice describing internal successful attributions to strangers. For example, tell someone at the store that you have a big speech coming up and that you can't wait because you've always been a naturally great speaker!

Conclusion

So what do Nicole Kidman and Albert Einstein have in common? Well they both have high anxiety and they both have gone on to success! Here are some more people have high public speaking anxiety:

Harrison Ford, Carol Burnett, Rod Stewart, Mel Gibson, Barbara Streisand, and yes, Warren Buffett.

References

American Psychological Association. (2013, December 23). Getting excited helps with performance anxiety more than trying to calm down, study finds. Science Daily. Retrieved June 9, 2014 from www.sciencedaily.com/releases/2013/12/131223083917.htm

Ayers, J. (2005). *Communication Reports.* April 2005 18(1). Performance visualization and behavioral disruption: A clarification.

Gallo, C. (2013 May) How Warren Buffett And Joel Osteen Conquered Their Terrifying Fear Of Public Speaking. Forbes Magazine. Retrieved from: http://www.forbes.com/sites/carminegallo/2013/05/16/how-warren-buffett-and-joel-osteen-conquered-their-terrifying-fear-of-public-speaking/

MacIntyre, V.A., MacIntyre, P. D. MacIntyre & Carre, G. (2010): Heart Rate

Variability as a Predictor of Speaking Anxiety. *Communication Research Reports, 27(4),* 286-297

Mitchell, R. K., & Nelson, C.L. (2007). Don't drink and speak: The relationships among alcohol use, practice, motivation, anxiety, and speech performance. *Communication Research Reports,* 24(2), 139-148

Chapter 3: Ethics for Public Speaking

Nestled in the city of Amsterdam in Holland is a house where Otto stayed. Otto had a family but his family had to hide from the police. If another family took Otto or his family in, they could be punished by the police. If you were the owner of a house, would you allow Otto and his family to stay there? What would you do?

In this section, we will look at the issue of ethics as it pertains to the speech situation. Ethics deal with looking at what is right and wrong, or fair and unfair. For the public speaking situation, it's important to know that the speaker is held to a higher standard, and if something unethical occurred the speaker is likely to be culpable. Public speaking is culturally contingent and situational. So, this discussion may not pertain to a American audience. As a speaker and an audience, use thoughtful judgment to ensure that you are doing the right thing.

Ethics defined: What are Ethics? Ethics is an examination of what is right or wrong. For public speaking, ethics is therefore what is right or wrong in the public speaking situation.

Public speaking ethics are different from the Public speaking effectiveness. You're choice to include an extra power point visual aid is a choice that one of public speaking effectiveness. But, if that choice was made and the image was one that was copyrighted then it becomes an ethical situation. Consider a speaker who discussed an herbal remedy but omitted the negative health effects, even though the speaker read about them. This circumstance is likely more of an ethical issue.

Elements of Public Speaking Ethics

According to Beebe and Beebe[18], one ethical area is that the speaker should avoid is plagiarism. The *Publication Manuel of the American Psychological Association* states that researchers should give credit where credit is due.[19] According to Northwestern University rhetoric scholar, David Zarefsky, Plagiarism is when a speaker "using another person's words as if they were your own."[20] For public speaking, a speaker should never present another person's speech as his/her own. In addition to the avoidance of plagiarism, also avoid plagiaphrasing. Speech Professors, Susan and Stephan Beebe, define plagiaphrasing as

> *lacing the speech with compelling phrases you find in a source; failing to give credit to a source or adequate information in a citation; or relying too heavily on the vocabulary or sentence structure of a source.* (p. 42)

In sum, the first ethical element is to avoid plagiarism and avoid plagiaphrasing. To do this, give credit where credit is due by citing sources. And, also don't misrepresent what the original author is claiming.

---

[18] Beebe, S.A & Beebe, S.J. (2012). *Public Speaking: An audience-centered approach.* San Francisco, CA: Allyn & Bacon

[19] *Publication Manual of the American Psychological Association* (6th edition). Washington DC: American Psychological Association.

[20] Zarefsky, D. (2012). *Public Speaking: Strategies for Success.*, San Francisco, CA: Allyn & Bacon

In public speaking, citing sources avoids plagiarism but also serves a strong function of evidence. So citing sources will move your speech from an opinion speech to a more well supported informative speech.

Citing Sources

How does one cite a source in a speech? To cite a source, state these things:

1. The point you want to make
2. The source (the name of the publication or place you retrieved findings from)
3. The nature of the source (depending on the nature of the source, if the source or authors are funded by an advocacy group or if there may be some conflict of interest state that conflict here). Most periodicals and large scale newspapers do not require this. Most online sources or multimedia sources do require this.
4. The authors and their related credibility
5. The date of the source
6. The findings of the source
7. Restate the point you want to make

At the very least, cite the source and date, although the seven point oral citation is to establish strong evidence and to completely avoid plagiarizing, further, it is to help the audience gage the evidence better.

Sample Oral Citation

Everywhere you look these days, there seems to be a call to fix education. While these may be noble goals, education starts at home and so we should dispel myths and stress recent research that can help the parent know what to do. So, should a parent use tough love or should they encourage? The Hispanic Journal of Behavioral Sciences, uncovered something important about encouragement. Jasmine Mena, an Assistant Professor of Psychology, at The University of Rhode Island reported her November 11, 2011 study.[21] Mena found that for Hispanic students, those who perceived their parents as providing educational encouragement, expectations, and monitoring had stronger positive beliefs about school and intentions to preserver academically." Mena also cites the importance of increased communication and extracurricular activities to help Hispanic students persist through school. So as far as recent on parental encouragement— there's solid evidence that that works.

Plagiarism and the Internet

Professor Stephan Lucas highlights some keys to avoid plagiarism while on the Internet.[22]

According to Lucas, when viewing Internet sites keep a record of (1) The title of the Internet document, (2) The author or organization responsible for the document, (3) the date on which the document was last updated, (4) the date on which you accessed.

---

[21] Mena, J.A. (2011). Latino parent Home-based practices that bolster student academic persistence. *Hispanic Journal of Behavioral Sciences, 33,* 490-506. doi: 10.1177/0739986311422897

[22] Lucas, S. (2012). *The Art of Public Speaking.* New York, NY: McGraw Hill

Giving credit where credit is due: citing sources

Everywhere you look these days, there seems to be a call to fix education. While these may be noble goals, education starts at home and so we should dispel myths and stress recent research that can help the parent know what to do. So, should a parent use tough love or should they encourage
1

The Hispanic Journal of Behavioral Sciences, uncovered something important about encouragement.
2

Jasmine Mena, an Assistant Professor of Psychology, at The University of Rhode Island reported her November 11, 2011 study.
3 and 4

Mena found that for Hispanic students, those who perceived their parents as providing educational encouragement, expectations, and monitoring had stronger positive beliefs about school and intentions to preserver academically." Mena also cites the importance of increased communication and extracurricular activities to help Hispanic students persist through school
5

So as far as recent on parental encouragement—there's solid evidence that that works.
6

It may be the case, that you have retrieved evidence online and are citing information based on a secondary source. Here's an example:

So, should a parent push their child to excel at all costs? On January 10th of this year, Science Daily highlighted Desiree Baolian Qin's research.[23] Qin is an assistant professor of department of Human Development and Family at Michigan State University. Qin's research will be published in a forthcoming issue in the Journal of Adolescence. She found that high achieving Chinese students were more depressed and anxious than their White counterparts. Qin summarizes her study by saying that having high expectations is fine, it's the way that we communicate those expectations. Specifically, the communication should be done "in a warm and loving family environment."

Another element comes from Zarefsky (2012), it is that we should be concern for the consequences of our speech. If you were to advocate that the audience do something, imagine that the audience actually did do it. Imagine a speaker urging their audience members to take Kava Kava Root to help ease anxiety for public speaking. What if an audience member did take you up, only later to find out that he/she now had liver problems because of the Kava Kava Root. This violates speaker ethics because the speaker was not concerned about the consequences.

---

[23] Michigan State University (2012, January 10). 'Tiger mothers' should tame parenting approach, expert says. *Science Daily*. Retrieved January 16, 2012, from http://www.sciencedaily.com/releases/2012/01/120110114525.htm

Another ethical issue is to be concerned about audience safety. There are two dimensions to this (1) physical safety, and (2) psychological safety. For physical safety, as a speaker, you are the person in charge in most cases and the audience will tend to trust you. This means that the speaker must be responsible for keeping the audience safe. Try to be concerned and observant in keeping the audience safe and you will remain ethical. If you are outside, this means that you the speaker, should find a place where the audience will not get sunburned. If you are conducting a speech on how a special football play, you will make sure you give the audience a water break. If you are in the classroom, and you have brought in an object for demonstrating, say a police taser, you will make sure no one gets hurt. For each topic and circumstance, you should anticipate the possible safety issues and coordinate the speech to keep the audience safe. Here's some scenarios for analysis:

- Your teaching a group of 15 elementary children about basketball at a local park. What should you do?
- You are speaking to a group of High School freshman and some in the back are passing notes and disrupting your speech. What should you do?
- You are about to present a class project, your friend was telling you about his class project idea, since you are presenting first, should you just use his idea?
- You are informing the class on tattoos. Should you bring in a tattoo gun and pass it around to class?
- You are speaking about a controversial topic you know there is some key research against what you are saying. Should you mention it?
- You are great at getting the audience to use their emotions to make decisions. Should you rely on phrases that will feed the audience's emotions?
- Should you say something mean to get the audience to do something good? For instance, belittle the audience to work harder to get them to actually work harder?

In terms of psychological/emotional safety, the speaker should not belittle audience members or embarrass them. The speaker should be very careful not to disclose personal or private information about the audience without first getting the audience members consent. Interestingly, some research indicates that audience members will disrupt the speaker is they have found that the speaker has belittled him/her. The research on this matter, finds that if the audience feels that if the speaker is like-able and respects you, the audience will try to avoid disrupting the speaker. In sum, always save face for the audience members and abide by the old adage: Respect the audience and they will respect you back.

Another ethical element is a speaker should be concerned about being culturally sensitive. That means be concerned about pathos-oriented topics such as race, religion, etc. There have been speakers who have dismissed these concerns as being "politically correct" and just gone forth. But these speakers usually end up coming off as stereotyping and end up decreasing their credibility. Instead approach the topic with concern, especially making sure your language and perspective are appropriate for the situation. Although this may be an American value, race and culture convey strong emotions so use terms that don't escalate the audiences emotions on the issue.

There are other ethical issues, such as the requirement to be honest, the requirement to not go overtime, and the requirement to allow the audience enough exposure to an issue. But the key elements are these:

1. Avoid plagiarism by giving credit where credit is due, and avoiding distorting the meaning of the cited information

2. Be concerned for the consequences of the speech by being responsible for the accuracy of your statements

3. Be concerned about audience safety (physical and psychological/emotional)

4. Be culturally sensitive

Ethical listening

As a listener, or audience member, you should also abide by ethical behavior. Here are some ethical guidelines:

1. Maintain the Free and Open expression of ideas. This means that you hear the speaker out, even if you disagree.

2. Be courteous and attentive. This means that you should turn off your cell phone and listen to the speaker.

3. To the best of your ability, avoid prejudging the speaker. This means, you are as careful as possible to not distort the message based on stereotypes and pre-judgments of the speaker and issues in the speech.

Thus far we have looked at broad issues regarding the speech situation. But is it ethical to speak up or to stay silent? As a student of speech, you are developing skills that set you apart from the vast majority of people. As Spiderman's uncle said, with great power comes great responsibility. Yes, you will become, if not already a super hero whose power is your rhetoric. So, what rhetorical ethical obligations or responsibility do you have. McCroskey (2006) outlines some important foci of ethical obligations in a free society, they are:

1. **To speak:** you have an ethical responsibility to speak up for what is right. As McCroskey notes, "When you see injustice or wrong being perpetrated upon other individuals it is your obligation to speak out against it" (p 301). Further we should speak well. Merely speaking is not enough, we are obligated as members of a free society to use all our power of persuasion, and to ensure that right wins out over wrong.

2. **Not to speak:** In many cases silence is the most ethical act. We should not speak if we are not certain as to the rightness of the situation.

To listen: If we do not listen, we may inadvertently support bad things in society. Hence, we have a responsibility to listen to and read from others so we can ensure we are advocating for what is right and just.

Conclusion

As a public speaker and as a listener of public speaking it's vital that you practice ethical behavior. Let's now return to the story of Otto. What would you do in this situation? What did he do? Otto Frank returned to the house where his house in Amsterdam where his two daughters and wife were. The Nazis had found them and killed them. He was given a diary of what one of his daughters, Anne, had written. He decided to publish it, you may have heard of it *The Diary of Anne Frank*. He also helped create a foundation to preserve the house where they were in hiding. If you visit the Anne Frank House, the last room featured a set of thought provoking ethical issues. But ultimately the house is a reality check to a speaker, Adolf Hitler who engaged his audience's emotions and created a climate of hatred and state sponsored genocide. Otto Frank's story, is a reminder that we as speaker's need to ensure that we are speaking with ethical narratives, and as listener's we are listening and reacting in ethical ways.

Chapter 4: Listening

Do you know what this Chinese symbol stands for?

The parts of the symbol are:

1._____

2._____

3._____

4._____

5._____

This Chinese symbol shows the complexity of listening. Sometimes the hardest part of listening is valuing the prior silent pause. Lakota Tribal saying: *"Silence was meaning-ful with the Lakota, and his granting a space of silence to the speech-maker and his own moment of silence before talking was done in the practice of true politeness and regard for the rule that, "thought comes before speech"*[1]

Defining Listening:

<u>**Hearing**</u> is defined as: **The _____ process of taking in _____stimuli**

<u>**Listening**</u> is defined as: The process of _____and creating _____ out of what is heard

- Miller's Magic Number: 7 +/- 2 chunks of information is human _____ memory capacity.

<u>**The main two types of listening are:**</u> _____ and Critical listening

<u>**Comprehensive Listening:**</u> **Listening to _____the speaker's basic message.**

<u>**Critical Listening:**</u> **listening to _____ or evaluate.**

Listening background

How often do we listen?

Listening happens a lot: **The International Journal of Listening recently [Jan 2008]** looked at how College Students Spend Their Time Communicating.[24] The team of researchers went out to see how students spent their time communicating. They found that undergraduates spent:

11.4% of their time WRITING

16.1% of their time SPEAKING

17.1% of their time READING

And _____% of their time LISTENING

So, most of the time are communication involves listening, including poor listening. For example, Public Speaking authors: Steven and Susan Beebe discuss students listening. They looked at a colleague's impromptu experiment, which found what students were doing at a specific time in the lecture. The findings were that:

___% were listening
20% reminiscing about something
20% were worrying about something or thinking about lunch
8% were pursuing religious thoughts
20% were engaged in erotic thoughts and sexual fantasies

___% were able to recall what the professor was talking about when the gun fired

Only 20% of college student audiences are able to listen to the lecture, and only 12% are about to recall the college level lecture.

Do we listen to recall?

Listening is one of the early parts of recall, namely it is the encoding process, recall is the decoding process.

Listening in education:

Does listening help you become a more successful student. Let's do an actual activity to see. So, is your listening competency helpful to your college success. Yes! Here's some empirical evidence: One study (Conoway, 1982): 400 freshman college students given a listening test at the beginning of the semester. After the freshman year, the 400 freshman student's college performance was looked at 400 college freshmen study:

[24] Holladay[a]; David Okeowo[a] International Journal of Listening, Volume 22, Issue 1 January 2008 , pages 13 - 28 DOI: 10.1080/10904010701802139

	Probation	Honors
By years end, students with high listening competency	__%	__%
By years end, students with low listening competency	49%	4%

Watson & Barker, 2000, also found a strong correlation with Listening Competency (ability) with college student success. Coakley and Wolven's 1991 study students with the strongest listening skills also had the _____ grades.

To listening effectively is to Listen Actively:

Principle 1: Prepare your brain and ____ prior: Get good sleep. Eat well. Exercise regularly.

Principle 2: Decide what you will be listening for/Listen Actively: Take Notes/_____ what is said/if possible ask related questions

Principle 3: Focus on the speakers verbal and _____message

Principle 4: Limit _____ (eliminate any noise/place yourself in a position where you can hear and see the speaker as best as possible)

In the Business context:

According to a survey of the fortune 500 companies, more than _____provide listening training for their employees. Further, Business managers rank listening as the communication skill most crucial to their job. And, research has shown that effective listeners hold higher positions and are promoted more often.

Peters and Waterman[25] in their book *In Search of Excellence* argue that a distinguishing characteristic of successful American companies is that they listen not only to their customers but also to their _____. An effective listening environment can boost _____ , increase cooperation, improve productivity, and educate employees[26] as well as reduce employee turnover and potential _____.[27]

In Healthcare:

In 2002 the American Association of Medical College (AAMC) added a competency requirement for graduate programs that included interpersonal communication. In addition, the Surgeon General's *Healthy People 2010* report includes 467 objectives focusing on improving the health of each individual, the health of communities, and the health of the nation by the year 2010 (Department of Health and Human Services, 2003; Office of Disease Prevention and Health, 2003). Objective six of this comprehensive set of disease prevention and health promotion goals calls for an increase in the number of persons who report that their healthcare providers have satisfactory communication skills.

---

[25] Peters, T. J., & Waterman, R. N. (1982). *In search of excellence.* New York: Harper-Collins.
[26] Mignon, G. (1990). Listening is a vital part of the communication process. *Journal of Compensation and Benefits, 5*(5), 308–311.
[27] Crittenden, W. F., & Crittenden, V. L. (1985). Listening—a skill necessary for supervisory success. *SuperVision, 47*(12), 3–5.

In the context of healthcare, listening is critical to professional competence[28]. The International Listening Association defines listening as the process of receiving, constructing meaning from, and responding to spoken and/or nonverbal messages.[29] Good listening skills have been described as:

1. maintaining _____ ;
2. giving full attention, both mentally and physically;
3. reducing barriers;
4. avoiding interruptions;
5. responding to the content and feeling of the message;
6. listening for ideas or themes;
7. conveying that the message is _____ (paraphrasing or restating what is said); and
8. responding to the message, both the verbal and nonverbal aspects.[30]

When effective listening behaviors are used, improvements in emotional health, functional status, and changes in physiological measures are reported.[31] Effective communication behaviors have been found to _____ adherences to prescribed interventions and recall of educational information.[32] For older adults in long-term care settings, being listened to is fundamental to their _____.[33]

The statistics contained in the IOM (Institute of Medicine): The authors of the report stated that between 45,000 and 98,000 Americans die each year as the result of _____. If the lower figure is used as an estimate, deaths in hospitals resulting from medical errors are the eighth leading cause of mortality in the United States, surpassing deaths attributable to _____, (43,458), _____ (42,297), and AIDS (16,516).

As a speaker, remember audience members will have various learning styles:

- Listening (auditory learners)
- Feeling (kinesthetic learners) and be physically involved
- Visualizing (Visual learners)

As a speaker and as an audience member be aware of how the ways to improve listening. What exactly does Perceptual distortion mean?

---

[28] Roter, D. L., & Hall, J. A. (2006). *Doctors talking with patients/patients talking with doctors: Improving communication in medical visits.* Westport CT: Praeger.

[29] International Listening Association. (1996). Definition of listening. Retrieved July 3, 2007, from http://www.listen.org

[30] Ceccio, J., & Ceccio, C. M. (1982). *Effective communication in nursing: Theory and practice.* New York: John Wiley & Sons.

[31] Kaplan S. H., Greenfield S., & Ware J. E., Jr. (1989). Assessing the effects of physician-patient interactions on the outcomes of chronic disease. *Medical Care, 27*, 110–127

[32] Ong, L. M., de Haes, J. C., Hoos, A. M., & Lammes, F. B. (1995). Doctor-patient communication: a review of the literature. *Social Science Medicine, 40*(7), 903–18

[33] Jonas-Simpson, C., Mitchell, G. J., Fisher, A., Jones, G., & Linscott, J. (2006). The experience of being listened to: A qualitative study of older adults in long-term care setting. *Journal of Gerontological Nursing, 32*(1), 46–53

Comprehensive Listening

I. Examples:
   A. listening to classroom lectures
   B. listening to get directions to a friend's house
II. Skills needed to be an effective comprehensive listener:
   A. ability to summarize information
   B. ability to distinguish _____ points from _____ points
III. Ways to improve your listening skills
   A. focus on speaker's main points
   B. develop note taking skills

Multi-tasking and Mobile Phones

Is multi-tasking good?

For optimum listening, try to avoid multitasking. In the Journal, _Brain Research,_ April 18 2008 p70-80, researchers looked at doing dual tasks, they found that talking while driving decreased performance by 37%. Even Listening to music can through off you're listening.

A new study from _Applied Cognitive Psychology_ shows that listening to music that one likes while performing a serial recall task does not help performance any more than listening to music one does not enjoy. **The most accurate recall occurred when participants performed the task in the quieter, steady-state environments.** Thus listening to music, regardless of whether people liked or disliked it, impaired their concurrent performance.

What's the impact of mobile phone usage on learning?

A study published in the journal Communication Education (2013) investigated the impact of learning on students when they were using mobile phones, and students who did not use mobile phones in the classroom. Those students who did <u>not </u>use mobile phones in the classroom were able to record 62% more of the information, recalled more lecture information, and scored a full letter grade and half higher on multiple choice tests. To improve your learning, avoiding mobile phone distractions will clearly help.

Uh oh, is your IPOD too loud?

Don't damage your ears: Audiologists Brian Fligor, Sc.D., and Terri Ives have identified safe volume levels for you to use in noisy places. Dr. Fligor, an audiologist and Director of Diagnostic Audiology at Children's Hospital Boston says, "Your typical listener is not at risk if they are listening in a quiet situation, but if they are in a noisier situation, such as commuting, they very easily are going to be at risk." Their study concludes that **80% of people listen at dangerous levels when background noise comes into play.** Dr. Fligor recommends leaving it at that **safe level of 75 decibels or below**, and investing in earphones that block out background noise.

Barriers to Listening

Speech scholars, Steven and Susan Beebe[34] identified several listening barriers. These included Information overload, personal concerns, outside distractions, prejudice, difference between speech rate (125 words/min.) and listening rate (700 words/min.), receiver apprehension, and focusing on delivery and personal appearance.

In speech there are some key barriers to consider in the public speaking situation. For the speaker, he/she should work hard to:

- Create a good speech: Create a well thought out speech, including having attention getting elements, and limiting the amount of distractions. For example, a riveting story or a visual image that helps the speech will go a long way in ensuring the audience is listening.

- Find the right amount of information, in other words avoid Information Overload. A speech filled with numerous visual aids will overwhelm the audience.

- Eliminate as many physical distractions as possible: closing the door or asking the audience to put away their phones are examples of limiting physical distractions. These are all great ideas.

You as a listener/audience member also can do things to limit the listening barriers. Some key barriers to consider from the perspective of the audience member are:

- Motivation: Many disinterested audiences need to be motivated to listen. Just because an audience member is looking at you, doesn't mean that audience member is necessarily listening to you. If you are that unmotivated listener, find a way to motivate yourself to listen. Ask yourself what you want to learn prior to listening to the speech. Ask yourself what information you need to get.

- Write brief notes: I think this is one of the most underutilized tools for listening. I've seen in many speaking situations, audience members doodling, or checking their phone messages. Try to avoid doing these diverting things. Instead, plan how you are going to write notes, and take effective notes. For advanced debating, where you must listen and respond to several speakers, note taking ('flowing") is a good place to start.

Flowing is note taking for fast speeches. It involves, chunking paragraphs into key words and phrases. It involves keeping track of who said what. It involves being able to record notes and prepare your own speech in a short time.

Listening for Evidence: A Case Study of Online Web Evidence

If you heard the following, what critical issues, perhaps even ethical issues, should students of public speaking focus on?

According to the think tank *Americans for Prosperity* "Environmental quality improves with economic growth and prosperity, so an overriding goal of environmental policy must be to

---

34 Beebe, S.A. & S. J. Beebe (2012). *Public Speaking: An audience-centered approach.* San Francisco, CA: Allyn & Bacon

avoid placing an undue burden on employers and entrepreneurs."

Although online access gives a lot of information, not all of it is unbiased. When evaluating evidence, sources can be biased. Hence, it's key that the audience is aware of those biases so they can make an informed decision. Many sources such as think tanks/institutes, radio/TV shows, and so forth may rely on noncritical listeners who default to emotions rather than their critical analysis. Always get background on the source.

The New Yorker (August 30, 2010) did an excellent review of how a biased source can disguise itself in their examination of the Koch Brothers and one of their think tanks: *Americans for Prosperity.* Started in 2004 by David Koch, *Americans for Prosperity* advocates for less regulation and less government oversight. David and Charles Koch own oil refineries in Alaska, Texas, and Minnesota, and control approximately 4000 miles of pipeline. They also own Brawny paper towels, Dixie cups, Georgia-Pacific lumber. The Koch brothers have a combined fortune of 35 billion dollars. The Koch brothers companies have been one of the biggest environmental polluters. Their lobbying and political endorsements support less environmental regulation and less government oversight. The Koch's political involvement has been intense. Based on public tax records, the Koch brothers, through think tanks, and lobbying efforts, spent upward of $254 million on lobbying and political contributions (The New Yorker, August 30, 2010).

When listening to evidence, it's important to analyze beyond a catchy title. Find out who is funding the source that we are relying on. Is the evidence supported by an unbiased source? Is the evidence supported by thorough research and investigation? Be a critical listener to ensure you're not simply advocating or opposing an issue without being duped by a catchy name or other emotion laden judgment. Instead, analyze the evidence and make a decision based on a thorough and fair look at all the facts. If the evidence is supported by a biased source, make sure you are aware of that.

OVERCOMING FOUR OBSTACLES TO GOOD LISTENING
adapted from David Zarefsky (2012) *Public Speaking: Strategies for Success*

OBSTACLES	LISTENER'S BAD HABIT	LISTENER REMEDY	SPEAKER REMEDY
Thinking is faster than listening	Listener's mind may wonder (daydreaming)	Concentrate on comprehending the speech main points; take notes	Keep the speech focused and organized; link each point to a main thesis (subject)
Listener's attention span is short	Listener stops listening to speeches that are long or complex	Build your listening capacity by practicing hearing longer speeches	Divide speech into small, compact segments. Add attention grabbing elements into the speech
Situations contain distractions	Listener misses speaker's point because of distraction	Concentrate on the speech message by filtering out distraction as best as possible. Try to visualize speaker's points	Prior to speech—create a good listening environment eliminate any distracting sounds, around audience chairs, etc. Stay flexible; adapt to situation.
Listener jumps to conclusions	Listener misses speaker's point because they distort the original message. Perceptual distortion occurs	Try to set prejudgments aside; suspend judgment at least until after you have comprehended speech message. "Listen to understand, rather than to respond."	Careful audience analysis (inoculation theory); extra effort on clarity. Avoid emotionally-laden language.

Chapter 5: Topic Selection and Audience Analysis

In this chapter, you will be introduced to the various aspects that determine effective topics. This determination has much to do with the speaker being aware of the Communication Situation.

Communication situation is defined as the specific time, place, goals, constraints, audience, and cultural climate that the specific speech takes place in.

For instance, here are several situations for evaluation:

1. A speaker is doing a comedy speech delivered at a 21 and over night club on a Friday night, two weeks before the U.S. Presidential election

2. A speaker is interviewing to an interview panel. This is taking place in the morning and there will be several other interview subsequent to the speaker's interview

3. A new employee sending an email to his boss on a problem he sees and trying to resolve a conflict

4. A family member speaking on a microphone to honor her mother on her birthday

5. A student speaking in a class of thirty students and to a professor who was the former speech team director

The topic you select should be in consideration with the given communication situation.

Key elements of topic selection

There are key considerations that need to occur to choose an effective topic. The key elements that take into account those considerations are:

1. A speaker's own comfort level with a topic

Public communication is different than private communication. A speaker is not required to give the most sensitive or personal of topics. In fact, speaking on a topic that is highly sensitive to you the speaker needs to be weighed out. Is this sensitive highly disclosive topic something you want to share. For beginning speakers, I advocate selecting something you feel comfortable with.

2. Narrowing the topic based on time and goal

What is the time length is a critical issue. Many novice speakers often believe the goal is the more the better, actually speaking too long often creates constraints for audiences, such as an interview committee having to stay after work because the speaker made them late. The speaker should find out what his or her time range is and not deviate.

Did you know that before Abraham Lincoln's Gettysburg Address a popular orator and former President of Harvard University, Edward Everett spoke for approximately 2 hours. Lincoln's speech was only 246 words and delivered in about 2 minutes.

Chapter 6: Informative Speaking

The most abundant type of speech! The broadest type of speech! And a speech that often misses its mark...But not for you!

Informing about a person

*Past person (appropriate for your class inform speech):

- To inform my audience about *Cabeza De Vaca*
- To inform my audience about the *economist, Milton Friedman*

Present person: introductory speech, a current famous person, a family commemoration

Notes:

- If you are doing a speech on a known person, make sure you give new insightful information.
- Use testimonial evidence for a person who is not famous (nothing has been written about).

Informing about an object

Often we inform on how to use an object (something you can touch), or what is the significance or function of a tangible object.

Object:

- To inform about *Maneki Neko*
- To inform about the *IPAD 3*

Informing type: Event, situation, or briefing

*Historical event (appropriate for your class inform speech):

- To inform my audience about the *Big Hole Battle* in 1877
- To inform my audience about *Mayan Prophecy of 2012*

Current situation:

- To update a tour group about a delay because a member became sick

Work status update:

- To update a workgroup about the current budget situation

Informing about a *Concept, Idea, Theory (appropriate for your class inform speech):

- To inform my audience about *Attachment Styles*

- To inform my audience about three theories of juvenile delinquency
- To inform my audience about the affects of *Turmeric and memory*
- To inform my audience about *Alzheimer's disease*
- To inform my audience about a *Buddhism*
- To inform my audience about effective child rearing in the US
- To inform my audience about dating rituals in South Korea

Notes:

Clarify abstract concepts to understandable concepts.

Informing about a process or procedure (possibly appropriate for class—see me if you have an idea):

- To show my audience how to Swing Dance
- To show the audience how to Kite Surf
- To show my audience how to play volleyball
- To show my audience how to use a new *computer program*
- To show my audience how to successfully *complete 2011 tax forms*
- To show my audience how to create their own *podcast*
- To show my audience how to get a high score on the Graduate Records Exam (GRE)

Notes:

In these speeches, audiences often need to complete something physical. These topics can be as simple as completing a form to as complex as learning an advanced dance. Work for clarity and simplicity.

Informing type: people or culture

*Past people (appropriate for your class inform speech):

- To inform my audience about the American transcendentalist culture in the from 1840-1870.
- To inform my audience about the *Tibetan* people
- To inform my audience about *Otaku* culture

Present people or culture:

- To inform my audience about the Chinese *Naxi* culture
- To inform my audience about *#ReGeneration* culture

Informative Speeches

STEP 1: Identify the speech parameters

Each Informative Speech is unique. Find the answers to these questions to guide you:

1. **What type of speech is it:** classroom speech? Competitive forensics speech? Job training? Coaching little league baseball? A symposium at a conference? etc.
2. **What is my time range:** 30 seconds? 4 mins? 3 hours? 4 months? This answer will lead to how much you need to narrow the topic.
3. **What can I use:** computer images? Sound? Lectern? Microphone? Physical Space?
4. **Who is my audience:** lay audience, expert audience, both; is there a key member (like an evaluator/instructor/interviewer). Children, adults, etc.
5. **What are any other considerations going into the speech**

STEP 2: Preparing your speech, yourself, and the audience

1. **Design a great speech!!!!**
2. **Dress rehearsals:** Do several run-throughs, choreographing the speech and polishing the speech. If possible, do a run through at the location   with all your technology, etc.
3. **Prepare you**: Dress to impress!! Dress to avoid distractions, Dress to meet the needs of the situation: sometimes it's appropriate to wear work clothes? Sometimes you'll need to consider colors that enhance videotaping?
4. **Prepare the audience prior:** should they be reminded to attend? To bring things to the speech? A schedule and outline? Etc.

STEP 3: Develop a draft outline

1. **Start draft outline:** brainstorm your ideas even prior to searching the internet. Use key words rather than exact sentences at this stage
2. **The outline should guide your research**
3. **Continue refining the outline throughout your preparation**

STEP 4: Develop Main Points and Researching

1. **Start with Main Points:** the Intro and Conclusion can be done last.
2. **Research:** Summarize the current knowledge (research studies etc.). Connect all the research to overall summations.
3. **Ensure accuracy of your research**

STEP 5: Use the best content: clarification, uniqueness and recall quality

1. **Include specific examples to help the audience visualize the key ideas**
2. **Simplify and translate information**
3. **Introduce new ideas and perspectives about your topic to the audience**
4. **Make the information as understandable and as recallable as possible**

STEP 6: Visual Aids and other complimentary speech tools

1. **If possible, include meaningful visuals:** Include meaningful visual aids (power point, etc.), audio, video aids.
2. **Choreograph the Visual Aids and other speech tools.** Where will you be at when

presenting? Will you be holding the remote visual aid changer? Should you ask someone to help turn on and off the lights? Etc. Consider diagramming if you have many options

3. **Who is my audience:** lay audience, expert audience, both; is there a key member (like an instructor/interviewer). Children, adults, etc.

4. **What are any other considerations going into the speech? Is this an understandable informative?**

   "If archeologists had done forensics analysis they may have discovered that tensions between the indigenous peoples of the Southwest were the greatest cause of the Anasazi abandoning their dwellings rather than the theorized cause of geographic weather fluctuations. Inter-relations about Mesoamerican people's needs to be accounted for in our theorizing of migrations."

Enhancing Audience Understanding

1. Speak with clarity: avoid fillers, project your voice, give clear descriptions
2. Don't overestimate what the audience knows: briefly define anything that can be possibly unknown
3. Use Principles and techniques of adult learning: connect to the audience members
4. Clarify unfamiliar ideas or complex processes: try a metaphor—"it is like..."
5. Don't be too technical: remember the art of translating technical information to lay audiences
6. Avoid Abstractions: compliment these abstractions with something specific
7. Appeal to a variety of learning styles: use a diversity of aspects to the speech
8. Personalize your ideas: include your own connection to the topic
9. Be creative!

Communication Researcher Joseph Chesebro's strategies to enhance audience understanding

1. Preview
2. Tell your audience how what you present relates to them
   a. Use personal terms such as "you" and "your" to help connect the topic to the audience.
3. Frequently summarize key ideas
4. Provide a visual outline to help listeners follow your idea
5. Provide a handout with the major points outlined
6. Stay on message with the topic
7. Avoid information Overload

Adult Learner Principles and Techniques

1. Provide information that can be used immediately
2. Actively involve listeners in the learning process
3. Connect listeners' life experiences with the new information
4. Make new information relevant to listeners' needs and their busy lives
5. Help listeners solve their problems

Enhance Audience Recall

1) Chunk (group your points) information:
   a) Verbally & Nonverbally
   b) Don't over chunk (information overload)
2) Help the audience visualize
   a) Give specific examples to clarify abstract examples
   b) Use a metaphor
   c) Use a summation sentence
3) Create emotional intensity
   a) Through your delivery
4) Motivate the audience
   a) Ask questions
   b) Use a questionnaire
   c) Encourage note taking

Enhance Audience Recall

1. Use audience participation
   - Particularly for demonstration/process speeches
2. Give the audience pre-speech information
   - Written, emailed, etc., forms in advance
3. Give the audience post-speech information
   - Send the audience a follow up message
   - Post the speech online and encourage the audience to review
4. Include interesting speech content
5. Eliminate interference (physical and psychological)

Chapter 7: Organizing and Outlining

Having an organized speech will help the audience follow the speech, help the audience recall what your speech was about, and help achieve credibility for you.

The Unique Speech Situation

Regardless of your future speech situations, remember one thing: your speech situation is unique. What's happening in the world today is unique to that time and place. There are things in the news that the public is talking about. But in a few months those news issues will change.

Even more relevant to the speech situation is that many speeches have very unique qualities. Many speeches are unique in that you will only do that particular speech with those particular parameters that one time.

You, as a speaker, are at a specific time with certain values and beliefs that are in itself unique to that situation. Even more significant is your unique speech writing process. There are many paths to creating an "A" level speech. And each of us has unique constraints to juggle. Some speakers like to write out there speech, some like to write out key words. Other speakers do mixes of both.

Discovering the Speech Parameters

To organize the speech, be cognizant of the situation and the parameters. You may take risks, but make sure they are well thought out and that they are calculated risks.

One parameter (boundary) is *The speech time parameter*. In other words, h*ow much time do I have to give the speech?* It's absolutely essential that your speech in timed out. For a 10 minute speech, the speaker will only be able to develop 2-5 main points. For longer speeches, such as four hours, or one weekend, or even 6 months, you will need to choreograph the speech with a variety of activities, and modes of speaking, visual aids, and so forth.

Another parameter is *choreographing the speech*. With multimedia and computer generated images, and all the other facets of the public speaking situation, the speaker should choreograph the speech. If it sounds like you are making a theatrical production, that metaphor would actually be very helpful. Some questions to ask are: where are you going to stand; and if you are speaking with visual aids will you move from side to side or just stand in one spot. This is all called "blocking" in a play. For a speech, arranging where the speaker will be during each section (blocking), can help you organize the speech.

Organizing the Content of the Speech

The content of the speech, in other words, what is said in the speech, should be highly organized. An organizational parameter for the content is *outlining or grouping the speech ideas*. There are three main parts of a formal platform speech:

The Introduction, the Body, and the Conclusion.

But outlining the speech comes down to simply organizing the sections of the speech, regardless of what they are. For instance, I might group the speech this way:

Welcome, and sign in. Cookies and special thanks, 3 key goals for the summer: A public speech symposium on health, (2) a speech contest for fitness trainers, (3) brochure development, Sign out and reminder for the next meeting.

Although both are different main areas, one thing in common is that both are chronologically organized, that is, each are organized from beginning of the speech to the end of the speech. So, the next *parameter is to chronologically outline the speech.*

You may have noticed two key things about the two speeches I've started to organize. First, they don't look like outlines because they are not spatially organized. Organizing a speech based on its location is actually a memory enhancement technique. It's called the mnemonic of logi. We'll just call this, outline format. The type of format relies on the speech being organized from top to bottom, with enumerated symbols, and spacing the words and phrases with indentation and style that make the points meaningful to the speaker. Thus, the next parameter is *put the speech into outline format.*

Our first outline format would look like this:

Introduction

Body

Conclusion

Our second outline format would look like this:

I. **Welcome and sign in**

II. **Cookies and special thanks**

III. **3 key goals for the summer**

    A. **A public speech symposium on health**

    B. **A speech contest for fitness trainers**

    C. **Brochure development**

IV. **Sign out and reminder for the next meeting**

As you're organizing the speech, one critical question will arise: What do I put into the speech? As you begin organizing the speech, you will need to effectively brainstorm ideas. Hence, the next parameter is *brainstorm what the speech should include.* Brainstorming requires that you suspend convergent thinking for the time being. In other words, try not to evaluate the rightness of the idea you put in at this stage of the speech. But your speech has only started to take form. This next parameter is where most of the work takes place and where your speech moves from a general message to a piece of art: you will need *to organize by polishing and editing the speech.* You will go back and forth, adding to the speech, deleting from the speech, and modifying the speech. The original brainstormed outline will be transformed, perhaps even unrecognizable by the final developed speech. During this speech development stage, you are looking for the best example, the best story, and ultimately the best way to deliver the most superb speech. You are crafting the content to move it from adequate to superb.

There are several main point speech organizational patterns. Five key types of main point organizational formats are (1) topical (based on the main point topic), (2) spatial (based on location), (3) chronological (based on time), (4) cause and effect (based on the cause of something and its related effects), and (5) problem solution (based on a problem and its related solution).

Important considerations for main point speech organization is (1) make sure the main points are divided into clear and coherent sections, (2) make sure the main points are somewhat balanced in terms of how much time is allocated to each

Transitions are going from one part of the speech to the next part. A speaker should do this verbally "Now let's explore our first main point…" And nonverbally, with a slower tone or pace that helps the audience understand that the speaker is going to the next section.

Outlining

Outlining = a written plan or map of the speech.

I. Functions of outlining

    A. Reduce anxiety

    B. Enhance memory through chunking (grouping)

    C. Gives the speaker more opportunities to edit

II. Effective outlines

    A. Organize similar points together

    B. Use indentations and space on the paper to show the importance of the points

    C. Use a consistent pattern of enumeration: Use roman numerals, numbers, and letters to organize the information

    D. Write in with clear simple points, to start with key words or write a more complete sentence form outline

III. Interesting research facts related to outlining

    A. Note: Did you know that cognitive psychologists (in *Science*, 1980) found that the human memory can remember from 5-9 digits, but through *chunking* a person can remember up to 80 digits (numbers).

    B. Did you know educational psychologists have found that good writers organize what they write more effectively than poor writers.

Outline format

According to the MLA (Modern Language Association) Handbook (2003), outline format is as follows:

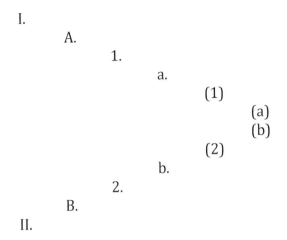

Speech Design:

Brainstorming based on your own ideas (Divergent Thinking Process): This is the process of coming up with ideas, and creating the possible points without critiquing. This is where some of your best ideas can come from. Don't take this lightly, if anything it will be illuminating to develop your own brainstormed list and compare that to research. Divergent thinking is creating or generating ideas, it is creative/thinking out of the box thinking.

Brainstorming based on research and information searches: This involves looking at ideas on the internet and outside of yourself. Probably the impulse is to do this first, but it's much better to wait and do this as a second step.

Editing the brainstormed ideas (Convergent thinking): This part of the process involves eliminated some of the brainstormed items. Convergent thinking is essentially critical thinking where one is narrowing down ideas to the best ideas.

Organizing the edited key words: This part of the process involves categorizing the long list of brainstormed ideas into categories. This organization becomes the body section of an outline. The main categories become the main points. The items become the subpoints. Essentially, this process is beginning process of outlining.

Enumerate and apply outline indentation of the categories and subpoints: This is essentially involves numbering and letting the points, and using meaningful indentation to organize the speech.

Finding balance for the content and making sure the main points are distinct are meaningful: This involves looking at how much information you have for each point, if you have 15 subpoints for main point one, but 5 subpoints for main point two, the speeches main point one may need to be divided into two points.

The Public Speaking design and delivery dialectic

The dialectic is *Oral Performance* and *Written design*: This involves the back and forth nature of speech. A dialectic is a simultaneous need. In this case, the speaker will sometimes need to write out and craft the speech and other times the speaker will need to stand up and actually say the speech.

Chapter 8: Language and Word Use

"No one knows what it means but it's provocative!!"
Will Ferrell, *Blades of Glory*

Language is such an important of your speech. There are numerous ways of saying things, you can say them metaphorically or figuratively. Think of the sounds that the words produce. Language use is a you speaking paintbrush and you are the artist. When you create a speech, you're making something that no one has ever created through the words, sentences, and images that you are creating. Make it count, make the speech language filled with meaning and messages that will move the masses with your message!

A fundamental part of public speaking is the crafting of thoughts into words. For simple messages this is easy. Consider the commands that we often use: "Pass me the pie," "Can you tell me what I missed in today's class." "I want to work harder on the next speech." But as a speaker begins to consider his or her speech goal, and the impact of the audience, the speaker should begin to select the best word use and sequence to achieve that goal. As a speaker, craft your speeches to reflect your desired goals as best as possible. Consider this, a speaker says: "Pass me the pie," the audience might consider this rude. Can you guess why? Yes, we've often been encouraged to put a "please" in front of our direct commands. Now the message becomes "Please pass me the pie." Next you may think, hand me the pie, would be better. But you've already had 2 slices, so you don't appear glutinous you say: Please, hand me the pie, this is my final slice I've worked out all day and I'm famished." We can continue depending on what your goals are and considering the entire context. The fundamental consideration of language is that the speaker crafts it to achieve the speaking goal.

Using words/language and all its sequences effectively refers to a speaker increasing the level of shared meaning with the audience, and achieving speaker's goals.

Often the ideas and goals that a speaker has is more complex then wanting to someone to take a simple action like passing over a slice of pie.

Different ways of phrasing a concept

To illustrate the complexity of phrasing speeches, what would you say in the following instances?

- o To motivate your team of 15 students to work harder to accomplish their final project?

- o What would you say to commemorate someone we have known for years at a conference?

- o What would you say to bring up a sensitive problem up to the city council without offending them but ensuring that they have heard your concern?

The crafting or the design of your speech often involves using language in original and creative ways. The best language use may be best understood as a great piece of art. Your speech will include a tapestry and color scheme all its own. What colors do you use, where do you place the colors, what mood to you intend? For a speech, what words and word patterns do you use. Does it convey what you want it to convey?

For instance, if you wanted to say that your are not satisfied with social justice for an ethnic group in the US? what would you say?

Here's what Martin Luther King, Jr said in his 1963 "I have a dream" speech:

> *We will not be satisfied until justice rolls down like thunder and a righteousness like a mighty stream.*

Differentiating Oral and Written Language Styles

Use Language that most accurately conveys the idea/feeling you are trying to convey

Use Language that is understandable, appropriate, and unbiased

Denotation and connotation

Denotation is the dictionary or literal meaning of a word or phrase.[35]

Connotation is the everyday meaning of a word

David Zarefsky, the author of *Public Speaking: Strategies for success* identifies several contrasting factors between oral and written style:[36]

- **Simplicity:** Oral style is simpler than written style. In oral style, shorter, more common words are used compared with written style.

- **Repetition:** Oral style is more repetitive than written style. If not overdone, repetitive style achieves several functions. First, repetition is a memory aid for the audience. Another function of repetitiveness is that it can highlight the main points and ideas. Finally, a repetition can function to help audience's understand a pattern in a speech.

- **Informality:** Oral style is more informal than written style.

- **Potential for Clutter:** Oral style is more likely to contain clutter. For instance, sometimes speeches include vocal fillers like *um* or *ah*.

According to Beebe and Beebe,[37] using memorable word structures effectively involves (1) using distinctive stylistic devices sparingly: don't over use stylistic devices, (2) using stylistic devices at specific points in your speech: stylistic devices should only be used at certain points in the speech where you want to make the point more memorable, and (3) use stylistic devices to economize: use stylistic devices to avoid the sentences becoming too long or complex.

Many speech scholars believe that language use should emphasize (1) using specific, concrete words, (2) using simple words, (3) using words correctly, and using words concisely

---

[35] Lucas, S (2012) *The Art of Public Speaking*. New York, NY: McGraw Hill
[36] Zarefsky, D. (2011). *Public Speaking: Strategies for Success*. San Francisco, CA: Allyn and Bacon
[37] Beebe, S.A &Beebe, S.J. (2012). *Public Speaking: an Audience-Centered Approach*. San Francisco, CA: Allyn & Bacon

Stylistic Language Devices

The following section identifies and gives examples of various stylistic language devices. In addition to adding more aesthetic quality to a spoken message, another value is that a speech that uses language memorably can help the audience remember the message.

Acronym

An Acronym is a word forming from the first letter(s) of a series of words. For example, radio detecting and ranging was the basis for acronym Radar (**ra**dio **d**etecting **a**nd **r**anging).

There are several other acronyms that you often use. Take a look at this passage and identify some:

> "I love watching NBA games, it's so exciting now that LA has several MVP worthy players, plus it's a great diversion from all the negative news on TV. For instance, I saw CNN do a report on guns, but the NRA will lobby against change so it's difficult to be positive."

> "I saw a great documentary on HBO. It was about PCs versus MACs. I told a friend I like PC's more, but she texted me this message 'WTF how about Iphones'"

Another example is when the Accreditation Commission wanted to account for what student learning. The Western Association of Schools and Colleges (acronym: _____) decided to require colleges to have Student Learning Outcomes (acronym: _____), but the California Teachers Association (acronym: _____) had concerns.

The challenge of an acronym is that the acronym may oversimplify the complexity of an issue. So, in a public speaking situation, an audience member should be:

- Cognizant that the acronym is likely an oversimplification
- Aware the speaker may not understand the complex issues when using acronyms
- Aware the an acronym may overly tap into emotional appeals

The benefit of using an acronym is that the acronym can simplify the speech thematically, this helps the audience remember the key issue (s). This also helps the audience simplify a potentially complex issue.

Cliché

A Cliché is an overused expression (Beebe et al, 2012). Although in most situations it's best to think of language that captures the point you want to make. Often that language is original and inventive. As long as a speaker doesn't overuse a cliché, the use of a cliché is acceptable. Writer's Digest (Klems, August 15, 2012) described that these clichés should be eliminated:

- *Avoid it like the plague*
- *Dead as a doornail*
- *Take the tiger by the tail*
- *Low hanging fruit*
- *If only walls could talk*
- *The pot calling the kettle black*
- *Think outside the box*
- *Thick as thieves*
- *But at the end of the day*
- *Plenty of fish in the sea*
- *Every dog has its day*
- *Like a kid in a candy store*
- *Tip of the iceberg*

Can you think of clichés that are overused? List some clichés that you often hear

1.

2.

3.

4.

5.

Slang/Colloquialism

Specialized vocabulary and idioms of those who share some type of similar subculture. Often time these words, are regional specific, and/or generational specific. When speaking, you may need to do some audience analysis to see if the audience knows what the term refers to, or define the term in the speech, or use a more understandable term.

Here are some examples of slang:

Sick: Sick doesn't refer to being ill or literally sick. It usually refers to something that was awesome, cool or surprising.
Hater: A hater is usually someone who feels anger or jealously towards another person because of their success.
Classic: Great
California Stop: Slowing down at a stop sign, but not actually stopping.
Bail: To leave a place
Psyched: Being excited about something
Bromance: Extremely close friendship between men

Metaphors

A metaphor is an implied comparison between two things or concepts (Beebe et al. 2012).

"All the world's a stage, and all the men and women merely players. They have their exits and their entrances" William Shakespeare

"Fiscal Cliff averted as Congress begins new fight over spending on social welfare programs" news title from *Democracy Now*, January 2, 2013

Write down an example of a metaphor if you were doing a speech on informing or persuading the audience to finish the class.

1.

2.

Simile

A Simile is a comparison between two things that uses the word *like* or *as (Beebe & Beebe. 2012)*.

"Life is like a box of chocolates, you never know what you're going to get."

"Busy as a bee"

"Your explanation is as clear as mud."

Personification

The attribution of human qualities to inanimate things or ideas (Beebe and Beebe, 2012)

"A computer once beat me at chess, but it was no match for me at kick boxing" Emo Philips

"She did not realize that opportunity was knocking at her door."

Omission

Leaving out a word or phrase the listener expects to hear (Beebe and Beebe, 2012). This is a good audience interaction technique. Anytime you leave out a word, letter or portion of the speech, it can lead to a nifty speech device.

It could be omitting a letter or word:

"Today, we (omit: are going to) win"

Omission can be a section of the speech:

"Today, (pause for audience to answer)"

Inversion

In spoken English the normal word order is subject-verb-object. Reversing the normal word order of a phrase or sentence (Beebe and Beebe, 2012). For example,

- "Ask not what your country could do for you, but what you could do for your country" John F Kennedy

- "It's not the dog in the fight, it's the fight in the dog"

Suspension

Suspension is withholding a key word or phrase until the end of a sentence.[38]

Parallelism

Use of the same grammatical pattern for two or more phrases, clauses, or sentences.[39] Bethel University library provides some good examples. Here's one:

Faulty parallelism: "My dog has warm fur, a nose that is wet, and a fluffy tail."
Take a look at the adjective-noun order. If "nose" and "wet" are switched, the sentence becomes parallel.

Parallelism: "My dog has warm fur, a wet nose, and a fluffy tail."

---

[38] Ibid
[39] Ibid

Need more explanation, see
http://library.bethel.edu/class/tutorials/writ-cit/Parallelism_in_Sentences.pdf

Antithesis

Antithesis uses parallel structures but opposing meanings in two parts of a sentence.[40] Examples of antithesis:

"Agree to disagree"

"Many are called but few are chosen"

"Ask not what your country can do for you, ask what you can do for your country" John F Kennedy

Alliteration

Alliteration is the repetition of a consonant sound (usually the first consonant several times in a phrase, clause, or sentence) (Beebe and Beebe, 2012) . Alliteration adds cadence to a thought.

Examples of Alliteration:

Discipline and direction   *Tiny Tim*

Confidence and courage   *Big Bang*

As a speech device, alliteration may serve as a catchy time and help the audience remember that the company or name or product. Here's some more examples:

- Company names: PayPal, Bed Bath and Beyond, Krispy Kreme.
- Sports teams: Pittsburg Pirates, Los Angeles Lakers
- People: Marilyn Monroe, Ronald Reagan
- Characters: Mickey Mouse, Donald Duck
- Products: Range Rover (car)

You may have used this stylistic device before, perhaps as a child. Here are two examples from one of the 362 nursery rhymes from Mother Goose:

Peter Piper picked a peck of pickled peppers;
A peck of pickled peppers Peter Piper picked;
If Peter Piper picked a peck of pickled peppers,
Where's the peck of pickled peppers Peter Piper picked?

The value of alliteration is that it makes it easier to remember the items arranged in a parallel pattern (Steven Lucas, 2012). When you craft your speech, consider the alliterative language use. The online source Rhetorician's Notebook has some examples, such as this section of Barak Obama's 2nd Inaugural Address:

---

[40] Ibid

Through it all, we have never relinquished our skepticism of central authority, nor have we succumbed to the fiction that all society's ills can be cured through government alone. Our celebration of initiative and enterprise; our insistence on hard work and personal responsibility, are **constants** *in our* **character***.(4:18)*

Imagery

Imagery is the use of vivid language to create mental images of objects, actions, or ideas.[41]

Repetition

Repetition is restating a key word or phrase in the speech. Martin Luther King Jr, uses this stylistic device frequently in his 1963 "I have a dream speech." Here is an excerpt:

> *...***Let freedom ring** *from the snowcapped Rockies of Colorado!* **Let freedom ring** *from the curvaceous slopes of California! But not only that.* **Let freedom ring** *from Stone Mountain of Georgia!*

Rhythm

The pattern of sound in a speech created by the choice and arrangement of words[42]

Onomatopoeia:

Use of sounds that resemble what the speaker describes.[43]   An example would be the sentence: "The cat meowed," "I bought a great patio set with the click of a mouse."

Audience Questions

Audience questions can create great interest in a public speech. But they can also open up the speaker to some challenges. For the speaker, if you are a beginning speaker,

(1) *use closed ended questions:* this is clearly a judgment call. But closed ended questions take less time and are easier to deal with than open-ended questions. If you have ample speaking time, open ended questions work really well.

(2) *be prepared for a variety of answers:* Sometimes the audience won't answer in the way you predict, you should be prepared for this.

(3) *state your question in a way where the audience can answer*: ask questions that the audience can answer in public disclosure.

---

[41] Lucas, S (2012) *The Art of Public Speaking.*
[42] Ibid
[43] Zarefsky, D. (2011). *Public Speaking: Strategies for Success.*

Not recommended	Recommended
"How many of you have ever ditched a class"	"How many of you have ever thought about missing a class"
How many have ever consumed alcohol and drove a car"	"How many know someone who consumed alcohol"

Open ended questions:

Questions that require elaboration in the answer, such **as "how do you feel about.."**

Closed ended questions

Questions that require a short answer, such as "yes" or "no" answers.

Humor and language

I spilled Spot remover on my dog. Now he's gone.
From Comedian, Stephen Wright

Try your hand at humor, write down two possible jokes, keep the jokes appropriate for a broad group of audience members.

There are entire books devoted to humor. Humor can actually be a very challenging part of the speech.

Incongruity theory and language

This is a breaking of a pattern, typically in threes

"I finally got accepted to a great school, but with all the tough homework, exams, and constant testing; I never realized how difficult traffic school was."

"for Valentines, I got her exactly what she always needed: flowers, chocolates, and a job application"

Freudian release theory and language

Sigmund Freud claimed that humor was a release of anxiety. Sometimes this can be used in speeches as well.

Quotations, Parables, and Fables

Quotations are statements from other people. Parables and Fables are stories with some underlying moral message or value behind them. These are excellent devices to use for opening a speech or closing a speech.

What are your favorite **quotations:**

1.

2.

3.

Do you know any **parables**? Identify them here:

1.

2.

Fables are short stories that illustrate a moral. Identify some Fables:

Putting cadence and language together

Many music lyrics include excellent examples of cadence and figurative language devices. Here is one section from a song from U2

Lyrics

The heart is a bloom, shoots up through stony ground
But there's no room, no space to rent in this town
You're out of luck and the reason that you had to care,
The traffic is stuck and you're not moving anywhere.
You thought you'd found a friend to take you out of this place
Someone you could lend a hand in return for grace

It's a beautiful day, the sky falls
And you feel like it's a beautiful day
It's a beautiful day
Don't let it get away

You're on the road but you've got no destination
You're in the mud, in the maze of her imagination
You love this town even if it doesn't ring true
You've been all over and it's been all over you

Take a look at your favorite music and consider all the creative language being used. Cadence is also an important dimension of, not only music but speeches as well. Cadence is the rhythm of the spoken word, including the pace, inflections, tone, even the word sounds.

Profanity

Speakers should avoid profanity while giving public speeches. When speaker's use profanity, there are negative perceptions such as being unprepared, sexist, uneducated, and unoriginal. What are some general reasons why so many speech scholars caution against this? What are your perceptions about a speaker's use of profanity?

Sexist and Racist Language

Speakers often over generalize and think it's a sign of bravado to alienate the audience through racist or sexist language, or sometimes they alienate/offend the audience without even knowing. I often hear statements like it's "politically correct" to alter your language to be inclusive. But it's not—rather it's inclusive and simply smart rhetoric to do so. After all, if you had a daughter in the audience, you would not like it if the speaker stereotyped all doctors as males, because you of course would want your daughter to be included in that possibility. Or when someone speaks about race and ethnicity, not only is it a sensitive subject but it involves families and family history of the audience. Use phrases and words that don't over generalize the audience or that don't alienate them.

For a detailed explanation of avoiding unbiased communication see the American Psychological Association Manual's section: http://supp.apa.org/style/pubman-ch03.00.pdf

Speakers should avoid sexist and racist language. What are some problems with sexist and racist language? What other language issues do you think a speaker and audience member may face in the public speaking situation?

Introduction Speech: 1 – 4 Minutes

This is a speech to introduce someone and welcome someone to the course. Gather information from the person that you are introducing. If your partner is absent the day of your presentation, you will do a self-introduction.

Preparation for the speech: Your preparation should include gathering as much information as possible about the class peer you are introducing. You are like a journalist on a fact gathering mission. Organize the speech information into 3 groupings, these will become your main points. Categorize the main points into short word titles—these will help you in generating a preview, transitions, and a summary. At some point, time your speech to make sure you are within the range.

The structure of the speech: For the Introduction--Start with an attention getting quotation, then introduce the person you are introducing, then give a preview. For the body: each of the main points will follow a format where the speaker does these three points: highlight the broad label of the main point, then discuss the point, then transition to the next area. For the Conclusion: summarize the speech (this is your preview in past tense), then revisit the quotation, then at the end of the speech, conclude by saying "So, please join me in welcoming a (insert adjectives) to our class. Ladies and Gentleman, please join me in welcoming (insert name)."

The content (speech material): Since you are starting with a broad categorical example, accompany that label with a specific example. A good litmus test of a good speech is the ability of the audience to be able to visualize what is being said. These vivid descriptions metaphorically paint a picture of the scenario and situation. For this speech make sure the material is appropriate, it's a wise idea to omit any material that the student you are introducing is uncomfortable with—after all the speech is about honoring them not a contest of self-disclosure.

The tone, delivery, and language of the speech:

Speak in a way where you build the credibility of the person you are introducing and achieve a tone on welcoming and commemoration. Elicit an applause for the person you are introducing as much as possible, and at least at the end of the speech. For language, as you start, avoid words that will make the audience uncomfortable such as profanity. Instead work to craft the wording in a way that captures the scene as best as possible. Try for good word use for all your speeches. Generally, most beginning speakers need to speak more formally and eloquently when they do public speaking—so challenge yourself to show your mastery of language.

Using speaking notes: Assume whatever you bring up to the speaking area, becomes a part of your speech. For this speech, you may use index note cards, if you bring them up they are part of your speech. For speeches without a lectern or podium such as this speech, if speaking notes are used, try the 3 by 5 inch or 5 by 7 inch index note cards rather than 8 by 11 paper. Write on only one side and keep them organized. Although you have note cards, remember your focus is still on the audience, so only look at the note cards occasionally.

Beginner's suggestions: This may be one of your first speeches. Here's some tips. Stay focused and keep your poise: don't go on tangents by talking about how nervous you are or say things that are not related to the speech.

Some content areas that you may want to ask are:

- o What are your partner's college goals (degree? Why your partner wants to learn the subject?)

- Where does your partner plan to transfer or transition to after Rio Hondo? (name the University or workplace)

- Where has your partner traveled? (Give about 1-3 places where your partner has traveled to and what your partner found so great about that place)

- What are some of your partner's talents/activities? (This can be specific hobbies or something that they do at work, languages, playing cards, dancing, etc.

- What is partner's dream job?

Sample Introduction Speech:

"The famous UCLA basketball coach John Wooden once said 'Ability is a poor man's wealth'[1] This quotation reminds me of the person I'm going to introduce you to today. I want to introduce you to someone who is an embodiment[2] of Wooden's saying. Let me first start by introducing this remarkable student. His name is Mike Gonzalez [3].

We'll take a look first at his academic and career goals, then look at where he's traveled to, and finally tell you what you can expect from him in the class and in the future.[4]

His academic goals are to get an AA degree here at Rio Hondo then transfer to CSU Fullerton for his BA degree and eventually go to UC Irvine for an MBA degree.[5] He is a computer whiz and his goal is to work on developing new technology in any field. Eventually he wants to work on his own, that's why he wants to get an MBA so he can start his own business. He has a lot of creative ideas. Like he wishes he could design a program that can help eliminate graffiti through the use of paint that uses nanotechnology[6], or even lighted hand rails for night students, he even said he could see himself designing the software for transportation systems, such as a monorail that takes Rio Hondo students from the lower levels to the upper levels. And really fast, so he doesn't have to walk all the way up the hill. He likes the exercise but already has a gym membership.[7]

So, now that you know something about his academic and career aspirations, let me tell you about his travels.[8] His travel has been done while he was in the military. He was in the Army for several years. It was there that he traveled to many places including Japan. When he was in Japan he saw this incredible airport out in the ocean, called Kansai Airport.[9] He thought it was a really great engineering feet. He also took trains that got him to the next large city by going 150 mph. He's inspired and motivated from those travels.

Finally, I want to tell you what you can expect from Mike in the class and in the future.[10] In class, you'll likely hear some interesting speeches from him, something futuristic. He likes technology but also is really practical, so you can expect ideas from him that are both technically advanced and yet have a real practical impact on your life. Imagine, a speech on a Robot that is really advanced, but then imagine that Robot washing your car while you're in class. That's the kind of creativity that you'll see. Beyond the class, the ideas he puts in play in the future will definitely help California. If I were to compare him to a famous person, I would say he's like a young Bill Gates, or Steve Jobs. But even better, since they haven't created a robot that can clean your car.[11]

So today, you've heard about Mike Gonzalez. You've heard about his academic and career goals, then some of his travel experiences, and finally what to expect from him in class and in the future.[12]

So when John Wooden said Ability is a poor man's wealth,[13] this idea fit Mike a lot. He's rich with ability. I'm sure if we looked into the future with a crystal ball—we'd see Mike having achieved some really great things. So, at this point please join me in welcoming an innovative and talented student to the class. Ladies and Gentleman, please join me in welcoming Mike Gonzalez."[14]

Notes:

1. Start with an attention getter that has a quotation or proverb
2. Use language that is more elevated than usual
3. Rhetorical technique: keep the topic hidden for a certain amount of time
4. Use Previews to highlight the main points in the body of the speech
5. Specific concrete examples help the audience visualize to exact point.
6. Use specific ideas and examples
7. Try some humor
8. Use transition sentences/statement
9. More specific details
10. Use transition sentence that matches your preview in order and wording
11. Try some humor
12. Include a summary of your main points in the beginning of your conclusion
13. In the conclusion, return to the attention getter to give the audience a sense of closure
14. For this speech, try to elicit an applause, vary your tone and pace to indicate you

Introduction Speech

Total speaking time: _____minutes

The structure of the speech:

1. INTRODUCTION

    a. Quotation

    b. Person Introduced

    c. Preview

2. BODY

    a. Main pts. were clearly labeled/identified

    b. Specific supportive examples included

    c. Transitions from one point to the next included

3. CONCLUSION

    a. Summary of the main points

    b. Restated Quotation

    c. Closing statement: "So, please join me in welcoming a (insert adjectives) to our class. Ladies and Gentleman, please join me in welcoming (insert name)."

The content (speech material):

   Specific vivid examples used.

The tone, delivery, and language of the speech:

   Language use: Formal enough (little or no slang).

   Tone: welcoming and commemorative.
   Elicited applause for the person you are introducing

Use of speaking notes:

Kept poise:

Avoided tangents:

Making Eye Contact

In this speech, there will be a focus on delivery: such as eye contact, stance, and movement; language use: such as specific details used; and organization: such as transition sentences. All this and you'll need to present the speech where you give every single audience member eye contact.

Eye Contact: Make *direct* eye contact with the audience members. Section this off by spanning from various audience sections. Imagine that each audience member wants you to speak to them so span your eye contact to them.

Segmented movement: Coordinate your movement with your transition sentences. This will help organize the speech as well. Make your movement deliberate but not robotic. Keep in mind, with the increase of computer generated presentation, coordinating the blocking of the speech will impact the organization of the speech.

Manage your body language: Your stance should be symmetric, relaxed, and confident. Your posture and body language should create your intended image. Generally, avoid hats, sunglasses, flickering your note cards, having your hair drape over your face, and even clothing that may distract from your intended message. Generally, for a classroom speech, dress in something that makes you feel confident and that helps the audience see you as credible. There are no absolute's for this area, so consider it and plan it out.

Language Use: Try not to speak too casual, you don't have to be overly formal, but consider achieving a good level of articulation. In addition, use vocal variety (varying levels of pace and inflections) and consider your tone to help communicate your message and organize your message.

Speech Content: Present clear details in the speech. Often you'll need to accompany your general example area with a specific. A good rule of thumb is can the audience visualize what I am describing. Stay on your topic—no tangents. You might consider the five senses (what did it look like, feel like, sound like, smell like, taste like) or even putting a metaphor in ("it was like…").

Transitions: Speak in manner where the audience knows when you are going from your introduction to your body then to your conclusion. In addition, each section should have some sort of transition that helps the audience understand when you are going from one section to the next. Transitions should be done through your paralanguage (changes in inflection, pace, and tone), particularly for the major transitions: "So now that you've heard of the three areas that will be discussed today, let's start with the first area.").

Organization: Speakers should have a distinct introduction, body, and conclusion. Further speaker's should have a preview and a summary. The speech should follow this organizational pattern:

Reducing Fillers (Vocal Pauses)

rev: originally from Gil Puga *(2002) Western Speech Communication Association Conference presentation "Using the Senses to Teach Delivery Effectiveness" p. 34*

You are to do a speech where you try to reduce the amount of vocal pauses in your speech. Vocal pauses are unnecessary utterations ("um's," "ah's" etc.). Throughout the speech work on your verbal behavior to attempt to have dynamic vocal qualities. Try to have a variety of inflection and pace in the speech to the point that is consistent with the feeling, tone, and meaning you are trying to convey.

At the start of speech include a brief pause and directly go into your attention getter. Use a preview. Your main points should be distinctive, and easy to visualize with a high amount of rich details. In the conclusion, start with a summary. At the end of your speech, try to indicate through vocal tone that you are concluding the speech. One sided note cards and coordinated movement optional.

Delivery:

Make direct eye contact, and span your eye contact to the audience appropriately. Your stance and movement should be relaxed, symmetric, and confident. Gesticulate naturally. Your physical presentation should not distract from your message and demonstrate overall preparation.

Vocal Qualities:

Avoid vocal pauses/vocal fillers in your speech. Use effective pauses and silence. Use effective vocal variety throughout.

Design (content):

Each of your points should be distinctive (clearly identifiable) and filled with a good amount of information that allows the audience to easily visualize your points. Consider what the scene/situation you're discussing looks like, sounds like, taste like, feels like. If the content is very technical or abstract, use a metaphor to help the audience visualize ("I marathon was 27 miles, *that's like* running from here to the beach.")

Organization:

Use a preview in the introduction. Use transitional sentences throughout. Use a summary in the conclusion of your speech. Also, organize the speech with your tone and pace of the speech.

MECARF Speech:
Making Eye Contact and Reducing Fillers

Eye Contact (the ability to engage the audience with direct eye contact and spanning the audience)

Give good eye contact to everybody. Your eye span should be to as many of the audience sections as possible. Avoid: *looking down, upward, or just focusing on one person or one section.*

Body Control (nonverbal behavior, such as stance, posture, movement, gestures)

Your stance should be relaxed, symmetric, and confident. Your movement should be coordinated and flow with your speech. Try to incorporate transition sentences along with the movement.

VOCAL Fillers/Pauses (eliminate the "ahs" and "ums" from the speech).

Keep the vocal fillers to a minimum. Use silence and pauses to add intensity to the speech. Pace out the vocal variety so that your speech has a clear and compelling message. Avoid: *pausing mid-sentence.*

Language (the degree of language clarity, word use, tone)

Speak clearly. While we all have style in our speech, we need to be understood. Try to be articulate while still managing to have your own style. Public Speaking and Everyday Conversations have different sets of expectations. Avoid: speaking too casually or informally,

Content (Include vivid examples, stories, and the details in the speech)

Stay on topic and gave rich clear details on your main points. Your descriptions made the speech easy to visualize! Also, include an appropriate amount of content. The amount depends on how long you have to do the speech: time the speech so that you are within time.

Organization (Use transitions, previews, summaries, and even your voice to help organize the speech)

Deliver an organized speech. Design and deliver in a manner where the audience can clearly distinguish between your Introduction, Body, and Conclusion. Ideally, the speech should be created where the audience can distinguish the main points and the main parts of the speech.

MECARF Speech organization should be as follows:

A. Introduction

    A. Attention Getter: Personal Story

    B. Topic revealed

    C. Preview: Use some crafty main point categories

B. Body

    1. First main point

    1. First main point category

    2. Describe the first point

    2. Second main point

    A. Second main point category

    B. Describe the second point

    3. Third main point

- Third point category
- Describe the third point

C. Conclusion

    1. Conclusion's summary

    2. Final thought on the lesson learned/significance statement

    3. Go back to the attention getter and close with appropriate tone

Team Speech:
The "How to..." Demonstrative Informative Speeches

Objective:

To collaborate with multiple speakers in a small group setting and an effective team presentation. By the end of the presentation, the audience should be informed about how to do something. For this team speech, participants should meet outside of class as well, plan to have an organized meeting. Communication research (Lehmann-Willenbrock, 2013) has shown that unmanaged (free) social interaction in group meetings leads to poor-decision making, unnecessary conformity, and ineffective communication, thus this assignment's goals is also to ensure that your meeting leadership is productive and meaningful

Requirements:

Presentation demonstration

Each group shall include a hands on demonstrative portion, where the audience practices *how* to do something. The demonstrative portion is effectively showing the audience what you are trying to teach them. Therefore, you <u>must</u> have some form of hands on activity. For instance, if your presentation is on Swing Dancing, you and or your members need to demonstrate/show how to do it.

Presentation must not exceed the time range

Each group has a maximum of 20 minutes.

Member Participation

Each individual member shall speak for at least 2 minutes and each speaker must use a microphone. *Lack of attendance and lack of commitment and group interaction ability will lead to a decrease in your grade.*

Presentation coordination

The presentation should be well coordinated and organized. Avoid having one speaker speaking and the other four merely standing on the side in a disorganized and random manner, instead, coordinate where each speaker will be, and include a variety stage blocking and creative use of each member. Choreograph and script the entire presentation to make best use of the time. Speakers are encouraged to creatively deliver the information. How would you deliver this message: *To learn Martial Arts, you should start by learning kicks, punches, and block.*

Each team shall have at least two out of class meetings

At least one of the meetings shall be in-person, and one of the meetings shall be done via Computer Mediated Communication (i.e., Skype, Phone in conference call etc.).

A Team written outline

Each group needs to have one typed outline. All group members receive identical outline grades—so make sure you arrange to ensure that the outline is turned in. I would suggest having a lead author email a draft to all the members prior to the speaking date.

In the outline, include for part 1: the minutes (meeting notes). Use these headings: Members (roles), Meeting dates and times, What was covered. Also include part 2: The outline of the presentation. Outline of the presentation based on the sequence of speakers and sequence of activities. The team can organize Part 2 in anyway, as long as the outline is enumerated with appropriate indentation.

Team Speech Topics

1. How to successfully transfer, get scholarship, and/or recommendations
2. How to dance salsa, bachata, line dance, and/or swing dance
3. How to make sure your doctor's visit is a successful one
4. How to incorporate great technology into your life
5. How to keep safe when traveling
6. How to have a great relationship: from the first date and beyond
7. How to add romance to your relationship/marriage
8. How to effectively negotiate for real estate
9. How to have the best hiking or camping experience
10. How to lose weight and keep it off
11. How to understand your pet's communication
12. How to say the right things when managing conflict
13. How to learn a language
14. How to improve your study skills
15. How to improve your memory
16. How to improve your reading speed and comprehension
17. How to protect the environment and wildlife
18. How to create a successful business plan and/or small business
19. How to add an extreme sport into your life (skateboarding, surfing, snowboarding, etc.)
20. How to master Martial Art(s)
21. How to put Yoga and or Meditation into your life,
22. How to decorate/upgrade your home
23. How to protect yourself from the sun
24. How to be a wine expert (i.e., wine tasting)
25. How to learn to play music
26. How to successfully invest money

27. How to protect yourself from illness

28. How to avoid getting a cold

29. How to prevent identity theft

30. How to be more fashionable at any event

31. How to defend yourself in court (i.e., take someone to small claims, or fight a traffic ticket)

32. How to put more art in your life

33. How to use sign language

34. How to make a podcast and or a blog

35. How to sell things online

36. How to improve your nutrition in your life

37. How to sleep better

38. How to increase your energy

39. How to improve your computer skills

40. How to fight a ticket, or win a court case

References

Lehmann-Willenbrock, N., Allen, J.A., & Kauffeld, S. (2013). A sequence analysis of procedural meeting communication: how teams facilitate their meetings. *Journal of Applied Communication Research, 41(4),* 365-388.

Team Speech – Grade Sheet

The "How to" speeches

I.   Speaker spoke well (clear, organized, and made helpful points)

II.   Speaker helped in showing the audience how to do something

III. Speaker helped contribute to the group speaking within the time range

IV.   Speaker used the microphone appropriately

V.   Other comments:

Informative Speech:

The Speech

Design and deliver a prepared informative speech. The speech can be about an idea/concept, an event, a people/culture, a procedure, or an object. Student topics (conceptual or demonstrative) need to be approved by the instructor prior to the speech, make an appointment (in person or even online) to verify the speech topic and start the discussion of how to do that "A" level speech. Be prepared to discuss at least three topic ideas and each of their main points. Because of the wide variety of options, our meeting will help you to do that "A" level speech. True, I want you to select a great topic for you, me, and the entire audience; but I also want you to come out of our meeting motivated and clear on what you'll need to do.

Requirements:

- A 7-12 minute informative speech

- 2 authoritative citations included in the actual speech (e.g., "The *Journal of the American Medical Association*, published a comprehensive study on the effects of wine on a person's health, their August 2008 study, included over 1200 subjects, and the study found that the effects of red wine on lifespan were....")

- Use at least two visual aid images projected from the computer. If you are doing a demonstrative informative you may do use pre-recorded video but it should not be longer that 3 minutes. It's recommended that the student speaker do a run through with his or her VA's prior. Speakers are responsible for a quick set up

- If you do a demonstrative speech, you may need to physical demonstration and have the audience participate

- A preparation outline with at least 5 authoritative citations in reference section is required. These citations should come from reputable sources

- Index note cards (3" x 5" or 5" x7") are allowed

- Attire: business professional preferred

The Preparation Outline for Informative Speech

your name

Title

Specific purpose: "To inform my audience about..."

I.   INTRODUCTION
    A. <u>attention getter</u>
    B. <u>purpose statement</u>
    C. <u>preview</u>
II. BODY (MAIN POINTS)
    A. <u>First main point</u> (a short phrase or sentence)
       1. Description
       2. Example
       [transition to 3rd main point]

    B. <u>Second main point</u>
       1. Description
       2. Example
       [transition to 3rd main point]

    C. <u>Third main point</u>
       1. Description
       2. Example

III. CONCLUSION
    A. <u>summary of main points</u>
    B. <u>final dramatic statement</u>
    C. <u>reference back to the attention getter</u>

<u>References</u>
Five sources minimum (APA style preferred)

<u>Visual Aid (VA) Description</u>
List and describe each VA

9 Suggestions for Visual Aid effectiveness

Above all a visual aid should be meaningful. Think carefully about the visual aid's purpose and usefulness.

Notes on Visual Aids:

1. Whether you are using a poster board visual aid, a splice of a video recording, power point, or other types of visual aids, you will still need to keep your focus primarily on the audience. So be cautious about turning your back to the audience and maintaining eye contact with the audience.

2. Practice using the visual aids. Ideally, you should practice using the visual aid in the same location the speech will be delivered. At the very least practice at home. Empty classrooms are also useful practice areas.

3. Do not show your visual aid until the moment your speech refers to them, keep the visual aid covered until that moment. This ensures the focus will be on you (the speaker) until you direct the focus toward the VA.

4. Stand on the side of your visual aid and do not use the lectern/podium.

5. Be sure that the visual aid text and or pictures are large enough and clear enough for all of the audience to see. Write large enough and use dark text colors. Also, place the visual aid in a place where the audience could see it best.

6. Try to smoothly integrate your visual aid. That is, make your visual aid a key part of your speech by rhetorically introducing it. For example, instead of saying "here's my visual aid…" you might introduce the VA in this way "Here is a visual representation of the wolf population (uncover VA). What is most significant in this chart is the increase in these four states…."

7. In addition to introducing the visual aid, clearly discuss how the visual aid is significant to your speech. This is referred to as debriefing.

8. Don't pass any handouts out to the class before or during your speech unless you plan to discuss the handout in-depth throughout the speech. It's best to distribute supplemental handouts at the end of the speech. Because you may have significant time constraints to consider—you might simply place the material on a table behind the audience and ask that they pick up a copy on their way out.

9. Other types of props (objects) may be used if they aid your speech. Make sure they are large enough. If the prop is small (e.g., a small photograph), consider holding the small object in your hand while you show the audience by panning the object to the audience.

Informative Speech:
Finding a topic, creating main points, and crafting the speech

Public Speaking guidelines and parameters come in many forms. In a formal Public Speaking course, a speaker may be asked to construct a specific type of speech within a time range, and with a specific amount of sources (evidence), and including several other specific parameters (i.e., use a visual aid, start by introducing yourself, etc.,).

Finding a great topic and setting the parameters can be one of the hardest parts of public speaking. Outside of an actual public speaking class, you will need determine the topic and set up your own parameters. Consider for instance, that you have been asked to come back to your high school and speak about your college experience. A good speaker would start by getting a good understanding for the circumstance: who is the general audience, how much time would be used, is PowerPoint and/or a microphone available, and so forth.

So for this assignment, try to select an excellent topic, main points, and craft an excellent speech. Here are some parameters:

- How many topics/main points: For topic starters, brainstorm ideas and then narrow down. As you begin you can have main points for each of your topics. I'll give feedback on which one I like most. Notice, that if you are not in a formal course, you can run through the two topics and feel your own response (did you like one over the other?) or even run through the topics with trusted friends or colleagues.

- Main points:
  - How many? This depends on how much time you have to give your speech. For a 5-10 minute speech, 3 to 5 main points is a good amount. Keep in mind, you can always cut some of the main points later.
  - What types of main points? Informative is open to various formats. Here are examples: *What it is. History of it. Factors, Types, Applications on different cultures, Uses, Future applications, treatments, origins, practices, dangers, key events, stages, etc.* For informative you should consider grouping the areas and labeling with a label that encapsulates the main theme. Keep in mind, that this is an informative speech, as opposed to a persuasive speech. To avoid accidently doing a persuasive speech be cautious about proposing a solution. Generally, when you ask the audience to take an action you are doing a persuasive speech.

- Format:
  Topic #1 (including genre)
    A. Main point 1
    B. Main point 2
    C. Main point 3

Examples

Topic 1: To inform my audience about the human life span

    A. Current life span factors of humans
       i. Genetic
      ii. Environmental
    B. Life span differences across three countries (Japan, Mexico, U.S.)
    C. Life span differences for men and women across in the US
    D. Three practices that decrease life span in the US
    E. Three practices that increase life span in the US

Topic 2: To inform my audience about smart fabrics

    A. What are smart fabrics
    B. Material in smart fabrics
    C. Medical applications of smart fabrics

Informative Topic Choices: For this speech, find an informative topic that is really good (for you, the audience, and me). And a topic that is unique and very informative (as opposed to persuasive or an opinion topic or a topic that the audience already knows about). Listed here are some topic choices that would work. If you select an informative speech topic outside this list, consider selecting a great topic from one of these sources: internet searches, Science Daily (free online), Science News, Scientific American MIND, Psychology Today, or Consumer Reports on Health. Topics from Scientific American MIND and Consumer Reports on Health are at the reserve desk on the 2nd floor of Rio Hondo library. I recommend selecting one of these topics, but you may pick an alternative. If you pick an alternative it is a good idea to let me know prior, I'll help as much as possible for you to discover a great Informative topic.

Topic area	Introductory Source	Student speaker in order based on speaker order for this speech
The Influence of Fathers on their children	Scientific American MIND, Science News, May/June 2014	
Multitasking	Scientific American MIND March/April 2012	
Science of Love	Scientific American MIND Jan/Feb 2012	
Social Networks	Scientific American MIND Jan/Feb 2012	
Brain Fitness	Consumer Reports on Health March 2012	
Slowing the Aging Process	Consumer Reports on Health March 2012	
The brain science of Weight loss	Consumer Reports on Health November 2011	
Foods that help your brain	Consumer Reports on Health October 2011 & Scientific American MIND Jan/Feb 2011	
Are supplements really safe? Vitamins: are they worth it?	Consumer Reports on Health June 2014 and March 2011	
Health myths or truths?	Consumer Reports on Health January 2012	
Cognitive affects of being Bilingual	Scientific American MIND July/Aug 2011	

How to Train your Dreams	Scientific American MIND Nov/Dec 2011	
Attachment Styles and mate selection	Scientific American MIND Jan/Feb 2011	
Effects of Laughter on the Psyche	Scientific American MIND April/May/June 2009	
Science of good parenting	Scientific American MIND Nov/Dec 2010	
The psychology of competition	Scientific American MIND Nov/Dec 2010	
The power of persuasion	Scientific American MIND March/April 2010	
Myths about Pop Psychology	Scientific American MIND March/April 2010	
Brainy Ballplayers: Elite Athletes get their heads in the game	Science News , Jan 14 2012	
Standing Tall is Key for Success: 'Powerful Postures' may Trump Title and Rank: January 7, 2011.	Science Daily (online)	
Smart Pants: Computer Engineers Develop Clothes that Sense and Interpret Movements April 1, 2006 (Science Daily)— New "electronic textiles" could help monitor the activities of patients with chronic illnesses. Computer engineers have developed pants with sensors embedded in the fabric that measure speed, rotation and flexing, and send wireless signals to a computer. Researchers plan to integrate computers into shirts, hats and gloves.		
Robotic Fish and Robotic insect sized flying robots (micro-airborne vehicles)	Institute of Physics. "Engineered robot interacts with live fish." *Science Daily*, 8 Jun. 2012. Web. 8 Jun. 2012. And LA times June 9 2012	

Touch Therapy Helps Reduce Pain, Nausea in Cancer Patients, Study Suggests. Science Daily (June 26, 2012) — A new study by the University of Kentucky Markey Cancer Center shows that patients reported significant improvement in side effects of cancer treatment following just one Jin Shin Jyutsu session. Jin Shin Jyutsu is an ancient form of touch therapy similar to acupuncture in philosophy.	Science Daily (free online) June 26, 2012	
Moderate Coffee Consumption Offers Protection Against Heart Failure, Study Suggests. Moderate Coffee Consumption Offers Protection Against Heart Failure, Study Suggests. Science Daily (June 26, 2012)	Science Daily, June 26, 2012	
The psychology of online dating: "Dating in the digital world"	Scientific American MIND Sept/Oct 2012	
Brain training: "building better brains"	Scientific American MIND Sept/Oct 2012	
Unnoticed persuasive cues (i..e, priming such as subliminal messages)	Science News, May 19, 2012	
Military combat marks the brain	Science News, Oct 6, 2012	
The Science of How We Learn	Scientific American MIND Sept/Oct 2013	
The Science of Handwriting	Scientific American MIND Sept/Oct 2013	
The Science of Learning Math	Scientific American MIND Sept/Oct 2013	
The Science of Resiliency	Scientific American MIND July/August 2013	
How to raise a Happy Child	Scientific American MIND March/April 2014	
Electronic Cigarettes	Consumer Reports on Health April 2014	
Happy Child	Scientific American MIND March/April 2014	

Informative Speech Analysis

Name of person giving the feedback: _____   Name of the speaker: _____

Topic: _____

COMMENTS
For this section, focus on offering a well thought out and thorough critique of the speech. Analyze the speech thoroughly and write up your feedback here.

Positives: What did you specifically like about the speech? Identify clearly *what* positive aspect you are referring to. Also, *where in the speech* did this positive occur?

Areas to improve on: What problematic aspects arose in this speech? What do you think the speaker needs to on? Be specific, locate also where this problem occurred, offer a solution for fixing this problematic area.

How informed were you after listening to the speech? (Circle 1,2,3,4,or 5)

1	2	3	4	5
Not at all informed				Very informed

Were the Visual Aids helpful? (Circle 1,2,3,4,or 5)

1	2	3	4	5
Not at all helpful				Very helpful

Was the evidence effective at helping inform or support the information? (Circle 1,2,3,4,or 5)

1	2	3	4	5
Not at all effective				Very effective

Informative Speech Grade Template

The Topic: *The speaker should illuminate the audience about a concept, theory or some determined informative topic.*

- ☐ The topic was fantastic! It was new and informative speech.
- ☐ The topic did not seem informative. Make sure if you are doing an informative speech, you are teaching about something. Careful not to do a persuasive topic, or other type of speech. Careful to ensure that you are selecting a topic that is new

The Evidence: *The Speaker should support key facts and sections with published evidence or expert testimony. The speaker shall create a well-supported Informative Speech as opposed to an opinion speech or other type of speech.*

- ☐ Fantastic job with citing at least____ citations. Each citation had a source, date, authors with their related credibility as well.
- ☐ Need to work on citing evidence. Give smooth citations including a source, date, and authors along with their credibility.

Organization: *The speaker should have a speech that includes distinctive sections such as the introduction, body, and conclusion, within which the speaker has identifiable and easily understand sub-sections, for instance three main points to the body of the speech.*

- ☐ Great work with the speech organization. It was easy to follow the speech. Good transitions and sectioning of your informative message
- ☐ Good but try to organize the groupings of the areas of the speech more
- ☐ Needs work, the speech needs to be organized better. Work on using your voice to segue from each of the key main sections. Also, give the speech categories to help the audience follow the speech

Content: *The speaker should have a speech that has information that is clear and easy to visualize. The speaker should include were necessary examples, metaphors and explanations that make the content clear. The speaker should also include an appropriate amount of content and meaningful content.*

- ☐ Great information. The examples and scenarios you used were really informative. You provided understandable new information
- ☐ Good. The points you made within the speech were understandable but try to help the audience better understand your points. Try using supportive metaphors or examples to help the audience clearly visualize and understand your points.
- ☐ Needs work.

Delivery: *The speaker should present/deliver the speech message in a way that demonstrates good body and voice use. For Body use, although there are stylistic choices that the speaker can and should make, a good speech has delivery that compliments the message rather than distracts from the message. For the tone, use your voice to emphasis points, and to segue from one point to the next.*

- ☐ Great
- ☐ Good
- ☐ Needs work

Visual Aids: *The speaker should include visual image(s) that help clarify the overall message. The speaker should clearly explain what each visual aid means.*

- ☐ Great. The Visual Aids were very helpful. You also did well to coordinate the showing of them
- ☐ Good
- ☐ Needs work

The Time: *The speaker should edit the speech to be within range of the time limit. Speakers are encouraged to time the speech prior to presenting to ensure that the speech is within the appropriate time limit. Timing the speech also means the speaker can add to, or edit the speech in a way that uses the speech time effectively.*

Interviewing
An Introduction to the Professional Speaking Situation

Overview

1. Some experts claim that:
    a. 95% of employers require interviews
    b. The job interview, according to some employers is more important than your GPA
2. An Interview is a two-way street
    a. It's a forum for you to find out about the employer as well
3. Employers expect strategic communication but "favorable impression management should not replace the genuine exchange of information" (Kirkwood & Ralston, 1996, Communication Education)
4. Stress positives and strengths never volunteer negatives

Interview preparation

1. Research the employer and position
2. Analyze and determine your skills, strengths, weaknesses, and what you are willing to accept and not accept (e.g., travel)
3. Try to predict the interview questions and review predicted interview questions
4. Practice articulating your accomplishments
5. Do mock interviews

Interview mindset going into an interview

1. Dress in a suitable manner to convey a polished, professional image
2. Be the "best" you possible

During the interview

1. Arrive ahead of time—never be late
2. Nonverbals:
    a. Maintain appropriate eye contact with all the interviewers
    b. Sit in an attentive posture
    c. Avoid any distractors (pen in hand, noisy bracelet)
3. Verbals:
    a. Listen carefully to the question asked
    b. Ask for clarification or the question to be repeated if you do not understand the question
    c. Use clear concise answers
    d. Include specific concrete experiences and accomplishments
    e. Do not be too casual, for example: for avoid calling employer by first name, joking, etc.
4. General:
    a. Layer your answers (use previews, transitions, and summary)
    b. Be cautious of the inferences (connections) people make about your points. For example, what is the inference that would be made if an interviewee asked at the end of the interview "How much does the job pay?" or "How long is the probation period?" Possibly, the inference is that you're only interested in money, or that you want to do something inappropriate and you're waiting for the probation period to end. If you need to ask a sensitive question like these, then craft the message so that the interview is less likely to draw a negative inference.

Sample common interview questions with corresponding considerations

In an interview you can plan to answer common questions that occur. You can anticipate questions from specific fields. Here are some questions that the Los Angeles Times (April 2, 2006, p.g5) suggest you master because they are often asked

1. **Tell me about yourself**

   According to Allyson Morehead, president of Professional Diva, an employment services company in California, one should respond by covering four aspects of your background, early years, education, work history and recent career experience. Keep your answer to a minute or two.

2. **What are five adjectives that describe you**

   Dale Austin, director of career services at Hope College in Michigan, says "the purpose of this question is to see how well the candidate knows themselves." Austin suggest developing a list of 10-12 adjectives, then narrowing to six that relate to the position.

3. **What is your greatest weakness**

   According to Morehead, one should see this difficult question as identifying where you need training or guidance.

4. **What can you do for us**

   Morehead says be confident and "a bit egotistical" in answering this question. Discuss your record of getting things done, mention resume specifics or career accomplishments.

5. **Tell me about a decision you made in the last year**

   According to Austin, this is a question to see your method of making decisions.

6. **Where do you see yourself in the next five years or 10 years**

   According to Morehead, try to create an open-ended discussion for advancement at the company.

7. **Why did you leave your last job**

   Do not disparage your former employer. Work on phrasing your response in a manner that highlights the position as a part of your career path.

8. **What is the most significant challenge you have faced in the last year**

   According to Austin, you should give a clear understanding of the situation and three or four specific steps or actions that you took to address the challenge. Finally, indicate the result of the actions taken and the example should have a positive outcome.

9. **Do you have any questions**

   Seth Wulsin, a career services advisor at The Art Institute of California in San Diego, says you should at least ask when they are looking to bring someone is for the position, then you know the time frame to follow up with the employer.

Interviewing assignment
An introduction to the formal professional speaking situations

The unique public speaking situation of an interview often produces a lot of anxiety because the stakes are very high. The principles learned in a public speaking class will help you convey speaking excellence in this setting. Interviewing requires the speaker to use appropriate self-disclosure and communicate his/her competency and credibility verbally and nonverbally. Organizing your responses with previews and transitions helps keep your responses organized and ensures you won't forget important details. In a way, it's like a persuasive speech, you are trying to persuade the potential employer to invest a million dollars in your ability to do that particular job. This assignment will also prepare you for more professional speaking environments like an important business meeting. There are several parts to this assignment. The main part is the interview presentation itself. Parts 2-5 are written portions and should be turned in typed and organized using the subheadings below. **Staple all 2-5 parts together and turn in.**

1. **Interview presentation:** On the day that the interviews, you will do a simulated interview. Come dressed up like you were going to an actually interview, and be on time. The communication in the interview will be rated based on your ability to answer the questions in a timely and thorough manner. In addition, your responses should be organized and have a good amount of credible content. You should also employ credible self-presentation, appropriate self-disclosure, and the other areas discussed in class regarding this assignment. For this assignment, do not make up anything, represent what you are doing, or have done in a positive way.

2. **Index card:** Bring a 5 by 7 inch index card. Type your name and the job details that you are interviewing for . The job that you select should be the ideal job that you want, not an entry level job. The details on the index card should include: a job title, description, key skills for the job, and possible interview questions. You can make up the job title and description if you cannot find an appropriate available job description .

3. **Predicted questions: Five possible questions you anticipate being asked with a brief answer:** Predict the possible questions that would be asked for the particular position you are applying for. Write the possible question and a brief word-for-word response (1-2 paragraphs). The first question is: "Tell us about yourself?" This is a common interview question. The remaining questions should be *specific* to the job. Use quotations to indicate you are responding to the question ("I would take several actions in that circumstance, first I would..."). Note: consider actually asking someone in that career area for some probable questions.

4. **Questions to ask the interviewer (Five questions to ask the potential employer):** These are the questions that the applicant/interviewee would like to ask to the potential employer. These are the questions that come at the end of an interview when the interviewer asks "do you have any questions for us." You may not have time to ask all five questions, so asterisk your top 2 questions that you would like to ask.

5. **Five personal accomplishments:** List five specific accomplishments that you have done that by the end of the interview you would want the interviewer to know about you. These accomplishments should be measurable and factual about you ("I completed a...", "I'm in the process of..."). Use school and work projects to get you thinking of your accomplishments.

Interview Grade template

Interview Speech Presentation .... __/65 pts

Index Card.. __/5 pts

Predicted questions & answers.. __/10 pts

Questions for Interviewer .... __/10 pts

Personal Accomplishments.. __/10 pts

TOTAL.. __/100 pts

Chapter 9: Persuasive Speaking

To some degree all communication is persuasive. When we give a speech or even when we communicate on a very basic level we are, at least implicitly, persuading the audience to listen to us. In this section, we'll look at more formal explicit settings such as a more deliberate public speech where the speaker outwardly asks the audience to take a course of action. That said, persuasion also occurs with are simple everyday messages. As the Winston Churchill once said, when asked what his greatest persuasive speech was: "It was persuading my wife to marry me."

Persuasive speaking defined

Persuasive speaking is "the process of changing or reinforcing attitudes, beliefs, values, or behavior" (Beebe, Beebe, and Redmond 2012).

When a speaker's position involves the word "should" or even the word "could," audiences are usually being persuaded. Consider these scenarios:

1. You should lend me some money

2. You should watch the History Channel

3. You should not drop out of college

4. You should ask him/her out on a date

5. Could you watch my stuff as I step out

6. Could you write this down

7. Could you give me a ride to school

8. Could you drive faster

Because public speaking usually involves a longer sustained message, the persuasive goal is often more evident. Here are some sample persuasive speech topics:

1. To persuade the audience to vote for an increase in higher education funding

2. To persuade the audience to avoid high sugar food

3. To persuade voters to elect a certain governor

4. To persuade an instructor to write a recommendation for a scholarship

Raphael's "School of Art" (circa 1505 AD) source: Wikimedia commons

Persuasive Means During the Classic Period

Aristotle's means of persuasion

Aristotle's three means of persuasion: During the persuasive speech situation, consider Aristotle's three means of persuasive appeals. Aristotle (384-322 BCE) wrote about these three means of persuasion: Ethos, Pathos, and Logos.

Ethos: appealing to the audience by having speaker credibility

Pathos: appealing to the audience through the use of emotions

Logos: appealing to the audience through the reasoning in the speech.

Ethos

First let's look at the concept of *Ethos*. Ethos refers to the nature of the source/ethics of the speaker. Ethos is commonly connected with credibility.

What is Credibility

According to O'Keefe (1990), credibility is the judgments made by a perceiver (e.g., a message recipient) concerning the believability of a communicator (p130-131).

Competence/Expertise:

Trustworthiness:

Like-ability:

To enhance and increase a speaker's credibility, speakers should consider speaking to:

Enhance their competency

Establish common ground with their audience

Deliver their speeches fluently, expressively, and with conviction

Credibility: at the start, during, and at the end

Credibility is a kinetic variable that is changing. Consider as an audience, the first impression we have on a speaker in the first minute of hearing about the speaker. If you, as an audience member, were told: "the speaker you are about to hear was the top speaker on the college speech team, and the speaker graduated top of her class," you would probably perceive the speaker as one having high *initial* credibility.

Initial Credibility is an audience member's judgment of credibility at the beginning of the speech

Using the same scenario, if the speaker begin to speak and she stumbled over her ideas and didn't seem very fluent, it's possible your credibility judgment would change, and probably it would be a downward change. The change after hearing the speaker is called derived credibility.

Derived credibility is the audience member's judgment of credibility as the speech is delivered.

Credibility is probably best understood in terms of the credibility after hearing the speech, or even a series of speeches, for instance in a political campaign. The credibility impression you have at the end is called terminal credibility. For instance, Alan Greenspan was the US Federal Reserve Chairman for several years. He was seen as a highly credible leader and speaker. Greenspan had been a staunch advocate of the free market. The chair of the Commodity Futures Trading Commission, Brooksley Born, challenged Greenspan on regulating the market more. Then financial problems struck banks and free market under regulation. Currently, many would view Greenspan's economic leadership and credibility as much lower than a decade ago. And Brooksley Born's credibility has, well let's just say, some want her to become the next Supreme Court Justice or Attorney General, it has increased tremendously.

Terminal credibility is the audience member's judgment of credibility after the speech has been delivered.

Pathos

Pathos is persuasion through the use of emotional appeals. Have you ever been persuaded because you felt really sorry for someone—that's via pathos.

Logos

The verbal structure of arguments/the words, the connection among them, and their power to persuade. The rational, logical arguments that a speaker uses to persuade someone (Beebe & Beebe, 2012). Using logos involves using supporting the message with evidence and compelling reasoning.

Cognitive Dissonance: The sense of mental discomfort that prompts a person to change when new information conflicts with previously organized thought patterns (Beebe, Beebe; 2012).

How Listeners Cope with Dissonance (facing uncomfortable information):

1. Discredit the source
2. Reinterpret the message
3. Seek new information
4. Stop listening
5. Change their attitudes, beliefs, values, or behavior

Monroe's Motivated Sequence: The sequence of steps needed to motivate an audience to take action.

The sequence

Attention: keep the attention, especially for resistant audiences (note: disliked sources more pers. in this category)

Need: Establish a problem that needs to be fived. Use narrative evidence (personal case study/real life story) and statistical evidence (i.e., authoritative research statistics, etc.)

Satisfaction

Give explicit, easy to do specific actions

Visualization

Use positive outcomes is audience abide by your persuasive action/belief

Use fear appeals if audience doesn't abide by your persuasive action/belief

Action: Often reiterated in the conclusion

Audience types and related speech considerations:

Neutral Audiences
- Capture the audience's attention early
- Refer to beliefs that many listeners share
- Relate your topic to listeners and their families, friends, loved ones
- Be realistic in what you can accomplish

Receptive Audiences: audiences in favor of your topic
- Identify with audience
- Clearly state your speaking objective
- Tell your audience exactly what you want them to do
- Ask audience for immediate support
- Use emotional appeals effectively

Unreceptive Audiences: Against your topic
- Don't immediately announce your plan to change minds. Concentrate on getting their attention and keeping them listening
- Begin your speech by noting areas of agreement before you discuss areas of disagreement

- Aim for minor shifts in attitude from a hostile audience
- Acknowledge the opposing points of view that members of your audience may hold
- A two-sided message (promotes your side and addresses other side)

One-sided and Two-sided messages

<u>One sided messages</u>: **Messages that advocate for the speaker's side only.**

Consider an example of a city's cleanup efforts in its local hills.

"You should clean up the Hills, because seeing the hills without trash will make visitors feel better about the community."

<u>Two sided messages</u>: **Messages addressing both the advocate's side <u>and</u> the opposing side.**

Example: "You should to clean up the Whittier hills, it will make people feel good about the community. You may be saying we don't have the time, that's why I say let's put a sign up that says "Please pick up liter."

What makes a message more persuasive?

- Two-sided messages are generally more persuasive than one-sided message. The idea is giving the refutation to an argument that the audience will be exposed to is referred to as inoculation. The medical metaphor refers to already being treated to an illness that one may be exposed to later. The persuasive metaphor is the same idea, in that the persuader gives the counter-argument to a point that the audience will be exposed to later, consequently, the audience will not be counter persuaded since they have already heard your refutation.

- Messages that arouse greater fear are more persuasive than messages that arouse less fear

- Persuasive messages with explicit conclusions are more persuasive than those with implicit conclusions

- Combine narrative evidence (case study of an actual person) with statistical evidence (research study from a scholarly journal)

Conversion: replacing a set of beliefs by another that is inconsistent with the first. In sum, changing someone's mind by converting their beliefs

- Chip away at the edges of beliefs: Not attacking beliefs head on—working from the periphery

- Identify a pattern of anomalies: Pointing out exceptions. Too many exceptions will eventually call a position into question, hence, an increasing chance of persuasion

- Employ consciousness raising: Informing the audience about a problem or situation

- Seek incremental changes: strive for small changes

- Use reluctant testimony: testimony coming from someone who is advocating a position against his/her own self-interest. Avoid biased testimony.

Inducing a Specific Action

- Identify the desired action precisely

- Make the action as easy to perform as possible

Toulmin Model: Model that looks at parts of a persuasive argument

The primary triad:

Claim	Warrant	Grounds
Your opinion	[Reasoning]	Evidence

←inferential leap→

Evidence

What is evidence: *Supporting materials used to prove or disprove something.*

Types of evidence:

1. Studies published from a credible journal, book, or newspaper source
2. Testimony from a witness
3. The opinion from an expert

Using Evidence

1. Use specific evidence
2. Use novel (newer) evidence
3. Use evidence from credible sources (reliable/unbiased)

Reasoning

Reasoning is the link or inference between your claim and your grounds

"I think your happy, because your smiling."

    ↑   ↑

(claim: opinion)   (grounds: information to support your claim)

Notice the warrant is missing, this is because speakers don't often state the warrant. Can you guess the warrant (type of reasoning) for the above example. See if you can diagram it to help to the relationship.

Formal logic is the study of how conclusions are reached using structured statements. Deductive reasoning, such as that of a syllogism is a common form of formal logic.

Deductive reasoning: Reasoning that moves from general statement of principle to a specific, certain conclusion. Two forms of deductive reasoning are syllogisms and enthymemes.

A **syllogism** is *a systematic arrangement of arguments consisting of a major premise, a minor premise, and a conclusion. There are three types of syllogisms: A categorical syllogism, a disjunctive* *syllogism, and a hypothetical syllogism.*

Categorical Syllogism

Major Premise: All A's are B's
Minor Premise: C is an A
Conclusion: Therefore, C is a B

Disjunctive Syllogism

Major Premise: Either A or B
Minor Premise: Not A
Conclusion: Therefore, B

Hypothetical or Conditional Syllogism

Major Premise: If A then B.
Minor Premise: A will occur
Conclusion: Therefore, B will happen

Enthymeme: An enthymeme is a truncated syllogism.

More contemporary types of reasoning

Inductive reasoning: Reasoning that uses specific instances or examples to reach a general, probable conclusion

Using effective reasoning

Key types of reasoning. The following are some key reasoning and their related definitions. These definitions have been simplified to make the type clearer.

- **Generalization:** Using specific examples, cases, and situations to generalize about the whole class they represent
- **Causal**: Showing that one thing is forcing or leading to another thing
- **Literal Analogy/Parallel case:** Comparing two situations, one with the thing you want to examine and one without
- **Sign:** Observable things as indicators of something the observable thing represents
- **Authority**: Relying of the expertise of another

Avoiding erroneous or bad reasoning (fallacies)

Hasty generalization: too few or atypical samples to draw an accurate generalization

False cause: a misidentified cause

Single cause fallacy: assumes there is only one cause, when in fact there are a multiple causes working together

False analogy: an inaccurate comparison because the two comparables are not similar in key way.

Appeal to popularity (bandwagon): reasoning something is good solely based on its popular use.

Appeal to tradition: reasoning something is good solely based on its past practice.

Red Herring/Straw argument: tangental reasoning because a topic has been changed or diverted

Ad Hominem: reasoning based on the person rather than the issue.

False dichotomy: incorrectly assuming there are only two alternatives when in fact there are more than two.

Slippery slope: assuming and without evidence that an uncontrollable sequence of events will occur

Generating emotional appeal

- Use emotional language

- Develop vivid examples

- Speak with sincerity and conviction

Elaboration Likelihood Model (ELM)

- **Peripheral route:** persuasion attempts when the audience has not mentally elaborated (thought of) the specific topic, hence, the audience is being persuaded based on side issues
- **Central route:** persuasion attempts when the audience has elaborated (thought of) on the topic at hand.

Some peripheral persuasion routes (see Cialdini for an excellent review):

- Authority

- Perceptual Contrast

- Commitment and consistency

- Liking

- Reciprocation

- Scarcity

Persuasive Speech
Persuading the Audience to Donate to Your Charity

Let's face it, we have all tried to persuade people for money. Perhaps you persuaded your parents or family to help you out by lending you some money for school or a business venture. Maybe you are a sales person and do really on your persuasion skills on a daily basis. Or, maybe you are in the education or healthcare fields and asked for a grant. This assignment is to persuade the audience to donate money to your charity. After hearing all the charities from the students, the audience will select which of those charities to donate to, and how much to donate. We will assume that each audience member has $25,000 that he/she can donate in any way possible and in any amounts as long as the donations do not exceed $25,000.

Assignment:

Time range: 3-7 minutes. The speech time range will be enforced. Time your speech before to ensure that it is within range

Identify your charity: Find an actual charity that you want to advocate for. There are many charities online. Try http://www.charitywatch.org to see examples

Use a persuasive organizational format: Create a Problem-Cause-Solution, or Problem-Solution organizational format for the body of the speech

Use evidence: Include at least one citation of published evidence in the problem section of the speech. The evidence should include the source, authors and related credibility, and date

Include a multi-component solution: Usually, this involves two actions (e.g., "Let's look at two solutions. We'll look at a legislative solution and finally a personal solution"). A multi-component solution means you are asking the audience to take two or more specific actions. You should give a specific amount you are requesting and make it very clear what the charity name is

Create a word-for-word speech: Type your word for word speech onto 8 x 11 paper. Your speech should be in annotated format or outlined. During the speech, the notes shall function only as an aid. Speakers shall focus their eye contact primarily on the audience (about 90% of the speech)

Deliver with emotional appeals: Your delivery should employ emotional appeals. Consider including stories that the audience can emotionally relate to.

A polished speech: The speech should be memorized or very well prepared.

Language use: Language in the speech should be well crafted and void of vocal pauses and other disfluencies. At some point in the conclusion, use repetition.

Lectern use: For this speech you are required to use the lectern.

Outline for the Persuasive Speech

I. Introduction
   A. Attention Getter: Note the attention getter should be particularly strong. Use a narrative story of someone other than yourself.

II. Body:
   A. Problem: include both cited Statistical and Narrative evidence.

   B. Solution (Multi-component solution)
      i. Write to...
      ii. Donate...

   C. Visualization
      i. what happens if the solution is acted upon
      ii. what happens if no action is taken

III. Conclusion
   A. Summary
   B. Final Appeal to act
   C. Reference back to the attention getter

Sample Persuasive Speech

INTRODUCTION: "One of my favorite musicians in Neil Young. You may not have know him, but he sings simple lyrical music often very political. In his song "Ohio" the lyrics were: "Tin soldiers and Nixon coming, We're finally on our own. This summer I hear the drumming, Four dead in Ohio. " You may not know this as well that Ohio" is a protest song in a reaction to the shootings of college protestors at Kent State on May 4, 1970. You also may not know this but Neil Young also had an illness which I want to talk to you about today. Neal Young had Epilepsy.

Today, I would like to talk to you about Epilepsy. I want to first give you some background on the disease, then tell you about some problems regarding Epilepsy, and Finally look at what you can do by offering some solutions.

BODY: "Epilepsy is the name of the disorder when someone has seizures. According to the Epilepsy Foundation.org, which is a national voluntary agency dedicated solely to helping those with seizures: Seizures are brief but strong surges of electrical activity that affects part or all of the brain. The Epilepsy foundation claims that One in 10 adults will have a seizure sometime during their life.

According the Epilepsy Foundation, there are 200,000 new cases each year. There is currently no cure for epilepsy, but there are medications that help control the disease. "

The problem with Epilepsy

"The problem with Epilepsy is two-fold. The medication that prevents seizures is itself dangerous. For example research published in the July 22, 2008 issue of *Neurology* found that Epilepsy medication increases the risk of birth defects. This is particularly the case with the medication Topiramate. And, more recently, The *Annals of Neurology* reported on March 18

2009 that Anti-seizure medications may increase the risk of cardiovascular problems. There are several other problem findings, but as you can see finding the right medication to control epilepsy is itself challenging.

And to complicate it all, if an epileptic fails to take their epilepsy drug, they are at risk. In fact, in a study of over 33,000 people published in *Neurology* on June 18 2008 found that failure to take Epilepsy drug increased the risk of death by three times.

So, Epilepsy is in dire need of continued research on its treatment. But there is another problem. The public must be informed about Epilepsy.

For example, the results from the 2000/01 *Canadian Community Health Study* are important to recognize. This study was recently reported in the March 17 2009 online journal *Science Daily*. The findings are that the rate of depression is twice as high for people with epilepsy, and even higher for females and minorities.

These findings are important to be aware of if we are close to someone with epilepsy. Unfortunately, there are myths about those with epilepsy. The myth that people with epilepsy cannot function in society creates workplace discrimination. For example, the Epilepsy Legal Defense fund noted some typical cases:

· In Tennessee, a college student was told he could not attend classes because of his epilepsy and was told instead to take classes via the Internet.

· In Texas, a woman with epilepsy lost her job after disclosing she has epilepsy on insurance forms provided by her employer.

Clearly the public is misinformed about epilepsy. For example, people with epilepsy can handle stress. A study reported in *Science Daily* on January 1st 2009 from Tel Aviv University, where over 316,000 people were surveyed , found that people with epilepsy can indeed handle stressful environments. .

So, we need to be informed about the medications and the nature of Epilepsy.

So let's look at some things we can do."

Solution:

"There are two key things you can do to help solve the epilepsy problem. You can embrace both legislative solution and a personal action.

First, you can take legislative action. Ask that they continue funding for Epilepsy research and centers. This is particularly important since there are 7 new centers that were supposed to be built for treatment centers for Veterans. We need to stress that these projects should not be cut. So write to your Senator and Congressional representative. Tell them to please continue the funding for Epilepsy research. Senate Bill 3406 helped epileptics join in with the Americans with Disability Act but, we all have to ensure that can fund research and treatment for Epileptics. I'm asking you to create legislative action. Write to your local Senator and Governor. Tell them to please continue their support for funding of Epilepsy research and treatment.

There's another thing you can do. It's a personal action that you can take today. It's important that we give to important advocacy groups. In this case, I am asking you to donate money to the

Epilepsy Foundation. I am asking for a donation of $5000 from each of you, or to donate whatever you can. That money will go to research, education and to supportive activities for epileptics.

If you commit yourself to this, you can know that the world is going to get better because of your commitment. We can someday find that break through medication, and In the meantime, know that we are informing the public about the dangers and myths surrounding epilepsy.

If you don't donate, it's likely that deaths from accidents will continue. It's likely with our poor economy that funding and support for epilepsy will be decrease. And, people with epilepsy can be seriously injured or die from the disease or the medications. "

CONCLUSION: "So, know that you know about the complex problems and have some solutions it's up to you to help. Please contribute to educate and mitigate epilepsy. The time for apathy has passed. The time for action is upon us. Join me and many others in helping the 33 million people with Epilepsy.

As for Neal Young, I admire his political courage to challenge political leaders. I also admire him being able to have the courage and fortitude to do all of this while having epilepsy.

Persuasive Charity Speech: Grade Template   Time Range: 2- 7 minutes

Attention step:

_____ Started the speech with a statistical and/or narrative example.

_____ Tone was dramatic enough to elicit interest in the topic

_____ did not reveal the solution until later in the speech

Need step:

_____ established a need/problem that needs addressing.

_____ included published evidence with the source, date, authors

_____ the speaking tone helped convey the seriousness of the problem

_____ was able to connect the topic relevance to everyone

Satisfaction step:

_____ A clear specific set of at least two solutions/action was offered

_____ A explicit donation request was made

Visualization step:

_____ A good description of what would happen if the proposed solution **was** carried out

_____ A good description of what would happen if the proposed solution **was not** carried out; including fear appeals

Action step:

_____ A summary was given (optional)

_____ Speaker included repetition

_____ The speaker returned to the Attention Getter

Overall:

_____ Narrowed the speech appropriately: Met Time range

_____ The speaker followed the persuasive speech sequence

_____ Speaker used words and language effectively and eloquently

_____ Speaker elicited emotional appeals

_____ Speaker made it clear that this was a well prepared polished speech

Persuading donations to your Charity"
persuasive speaking through Monroe's Motivated Sequence

Your name:

I certify that I watched all speakers _____ (initial). If you missed a speaker, write "missed speech" for the amount given for this speaker. When giving an amount, do not put comma's or money sign. For instance, if you were to give $2,500 to a speaker, it would be written: 2500. Donors cannot give any single speaker more than 10,000. It's recommended that donors give increments of 2500, 5000, 7500, and 10000. Donors cannot give money to themselves

Speaker's Name	Charity name	Comments	Amount given

Persuading donations to your Charity" persuasive speaking through Monroe's Motivated Sequence			

Martin Luther King, Jr. – "I Have a Dream"
August 1963, The Lincoln Memorial, Washington D.C.

I am happy to join with you today in what will go down in history as the greatest demonstration for freedom in the history of our nation.

Five score years ago, a great American, in whose symbolic shadow we stand today, signed the Emancipation Proclamation. This momentous decree came as a great beacon light of hope to millions of Negro slaves who had been seared in the flames of withering injustice. It came as a joyous daybreak to end the long night of their captivity.

But one hundred years later, the Negro still is not free. One hundred years later, the life of the Negro is still sadly crippled by the manacles of segregation and the chains of discrimination. One hundred years later, the Negro lives on a lonely island of poverty in the midst of a vast ocean of material prosperity. One hundred years later, the Negro is still languished in the corners of American society and finds himself an exile in his own land. And so we've come here today to dramatize a shameful condition.

In a sense we've come to our nation's capital to cash a check. When the architects of our republic wrote the magnificent words of the Constitution and the Declaration of Independence, they were signing a promissory note to which every American was to fall heir. This note was a promise that all men, yes, black men as well as white men, would be guaranteed the "unalienable Rights" of "Life, Liberty and the pursuit of Happiness." It is obvious today that America has defaulted on this promissory note, insofar as her citizens of color are concerned. Instead of honoring this sacred obligation, America has given the Negro people a bad check, a check which has come back marked "insufficient funds."

But we refuse to believe that the bank of justice is bankrupt. We refuse to believe that there are insufficient funds in the great vaults of opportunity of this nation. And so, we've come to cash this check, a check that will give us upon demand the riches of freedom and the security of justice.

We have also come to this hallowed spot to remind America of the fierce urgency of Now. This is no time to engage in the luxury of cooling off or to take the tranquilizing drug of gradualism. Now is the time to make real the promises of democracy. Now is the time to rise from the dark and desolate valley of segregation to the sunlit path of racial justice. Now is the time to lift our nation from the quick sands of racial injustice to the solid rock of brotherhood. Now is the time to make justice a reality for all of God's children.

It would be fatal for the nation to overlook the urgency of the moment. This sweltering summer of the Negro's legitimate discontent will not pass until there is an invigorating autumn of freedom and equality. Nineteen sixty-three is not an end, but a beginning. And those who hope that the Negro needed to blow off steam and will now be content will have a rude awakening if the nation returns to business as usual. And there will be neither rest nor tranquility in America until the Negro is granted his citizenship rights. The whirlwinds of revolt will continue to shake the foundations of our nation until the bright day of justice emerges.

But there is something that I must say to my people, who stand on the warm threshold which leads into the palace of justice: In the process of gaining our rightful place, we must not be guilty of wrongful deeds. Let us not seek to satisfy our thirst for freedom by drinking from the cup of bitterness and hatred. We must forever conduct our struggle on the high plane of dignity and discipline. We must not allow our creative protest to degenerate into physical violence. Again and again, we must rise to the majestic heights of meeting physical force with soul force.

The marvelous new militancy which has engulfed the Negro community must not lead us to a distrust of all white people, for many of our white brothers, as evidenced by their presence here today, have come to realize that their destiny is tied up with our destiny. And they have come to realize that their freedom is inextricably bound to our freedom.

We cannot walk alone.

And as we walk, we must make the pledge that we shall always march ahead.

We cannot turn back.

There are those who are asking the devotees of civil rights, "When will you be satisfied?" We can never be satisfied as long as the Negro is the victim of the unspeakable horrors of police brutality. We can never be satisfied as long as our bodies, heavy with the fatigue of travel, cannot gain lodging in the motels of the highways and the hotels of the cities. We cannot be satisfied as long as the negro's basic mobility is from a smaller ghetto to a larger one. We can never be satisfied as long as our children are stripped of their self-hood and robbed of their dignity by signs stating: "For Whites Only." We cannot be satisfied as long as a Negro in Mississippi cannot vote and a Negro in New York believes he has nothing for which to vote. No, no, we are not satisfied, and we will not be satisfied until "justice rolls down like waters, and righteousness like a mighty stream."[1]

I am not unmindful that some of you have come here out of great trials and tribulations. Some of you have come fresh from narrow jail cells. And some of you have come from areas where your quest -- quest for freedom left you battered by the storms of persecution and staggered by the winds of police brutality. You have been the veterans of creative suffering. Continue to work with the faith that unearned suffering is redemptive. Go back to Mississippi, go back to Alabama, go back to South Carolina, go back to Georgia, go back to Louisiana, go back to the slums and ghettos of our northern cities, knowing that somehow this situation can and will be changed.

Let us not wallow in the valley of despair, I say to you today, my friends.

And so even though we face the difficulties of today and tomorrow, I still have a dream. It is a dream deeply rooted in the American dream.

I have a dream that one day this nation will rise up and live out the true meaning of its creed: "We hold these truths to be self-evident, that all men are created equal."

I have a dream that one day on the red hills of Georgia, the sons of former slaves and the sons of former slave owners will be able to sit down together at the table of brotherhood.

I have a dream that one day even the state of Mississippi, a state sweltering with the heat of injustice, sweltering with the heat of oppression, will be transformed into an oasis of freedom and justice.

I have a dream that my four little children will one day live in a nation where they will not be judged by the color of their skin but by the content of their character.

I have a *dream* today!

I have a dream that one day, down in Alabama, with its vicious racists, with its governor having his lips dripping with the words of "interposition" and "nullification" -- one day right there in Alabama little black boys and black girls will be able to join hands with little white boys and white girls as sisters and brothers.

I have a *dream* today!

I have a dream that one day every valley shall be exalted, and every hill and mountain shall be made low, the rough places will be made plain, and the crooked places will be made straight; "and the glory of the Lord shall be revealed and all flesh shall see it together."[2]

This is our hope, and this is the faith that I go back to the South with.

With this faith, we will be able to hew out of the mountain of despair a stone of hope. With this faith, we will be able to transform the jangling discords of our nation into a beautiful symphony of brotherhood. With this faith, we will be able to work together, to pray together, to struggle together, to go to jail together, to stand up for freedom together, knowing that we will be free one day.

And this will be the day -- this will be the day when all of God's children will be able to sing with new meaning:

My country 'tis of thee, sweet land of liberty, of thee I sing.

Land where my fathers died, land of the Pilgrim's pride,

From every mountainside, let freedom ring!

And if America is to be a great nation, this must become true.

And so let freedom ring from the prodigious hilltops of New Hampshire.

Let freedom ring from the mighty mountains of New York.

Let freedom ring from the heightening Alleghenies of Pennsylvania.

Let freedom ring from the snow-capped Rockies of Colorado.

Let freedom ring from the curvaceous slopes of California.

But not only that:

Let freedom ring from Stone Mountain of Georgia.

Let freedom ring from Lookout Mountain of Tennessee.

Let freedom ring from every hill and molehill of Mississippi.

From every mountainside, let freedom ring.

And when this happens, when we allow freedom ring, when we let it ring from every village and every hamlet, from every state and every city, we will be able to speed up that day when *all* of God's children, black men and white men, Jews and Gentiles, Protestants and Catholics, will be able to join hands and sing in the words of the old Negro spiritual:

> *Free at last! Free at last!*

> *Thank God Almighty, we are free at last*

Special Project Speech

For the speech type you select, the parameters are listed here. These speeches are rated on everything you've learned in this course, specifically: the preparation level, speech organization, delivery, clear and eloquent language use, emotional impact, well supported points, and overall effect.

Speech to Entertain/Humorous

Purpose: To use humor in a speech

- Deliver a very well prepared STE. This is like an informative or persuasive with humor. It should revolve around one theme.

- Time Range 4-10 minutes (note: flexible time limit because of laughter)

- Outline not required. Note cards optional

- Audience laughter will be noted. Adequately pause for laughter

- For this speech plan out your humor. Work on trying to include humorous episodes, stories, jokes, and nonverbals

- Avoid offensive humor (i.e., racist, sexist humor)

- Somewhere in the conclusion include a social significance statement, in other words, a serious insight into what the topic says about our society

- No visual aids allowed

- Example Topic: How to date on a budget

- Example Main points: How expensive dating is; How to get your partner to pay; ways that you can trim your budget without your date knowing you're the tightest person in the world.

Motivational Speech

Purpose: To inspire the audience to embrace an attitude, value, or belief

- Deliver a very well prepared motivational speech. This speech should be geared toward getting your audience to embrace a belief, value, or attitude.

- Time Range 4-10 minutes

- Evidence: cite at least 1 complete authoritative sources (example: "Marriage should be your main goal because it helps your health, in fact, Hui Liu, an assistant professor of sociology at Michigan State University, reported in the *Journal of Health and Social Behavior* on September 2008, that married people are still healthier than unmarried people.")

- Outline required. Note Cards optional

- Emotional appeals required (avoidance of monotone delivery is a must, instead at some points speak to have your audience emotionally feel your passion. Use vocal variety, increase your inflection, and so forth)

- No visual aids allowed

- Example Topic: Persevere through to your highest level of education

- Example Main points might be: Don't give up on your talent for money; Commit to your education; Go for your highest educational degree

Commemorative Speech

Purpose: To recognize and appreciate a person

- Deliver a very well prepared commemorative speech. This is a speech to honor someone (someone you know or a historical figure).

- Time Range 4-10 minutes

- Evidence: cite at least 3 complete opinion/testimony sources (i.e., "my grandmother is an incredibly friendly person, according to her husband of 30 years 'she could make friends with anyone'")

- Outline required. Note Cards optional

- Visual aid required (show images via computer projection such as power point)

- The speech should include a commemorative tone, and include in the conclusion a part about what the commemorated person's legacy was (what lessons did he/she teach us)

- Example Topic: To recognize and appreciate my grandmother

- Example Main points might be: Her early life experiences, Her sense of humor, and Her commitment to family

Other

per instructor consultation and permission

Do you have some specific type of speech that you would like to do other than the three types of speeches that are identified here? If so, it may be possible to do it as a *Special Project Speech.* Please see your instructor in advance of the speech to develop the parameters.

Speech to Entertain

Speaker:

Total time: (Note: 4-10 mins. with a 2 minute grace period)

Scale: 1-5 rating. (5 is the top A+ rating, 1 is the lowest rating)

_____ Overall, the speech exemplified your thorough understanding and application of things we have covered in class.

_____ _Content:_ Overall the speech was really humorous. Good creative humor use.

_____ _Organization:_ Good preview, summary, and transitions. The speech was easy to follow.

_____ _Delivery:_ Good at using all those things from class: good eye contact, stance. Also good word use—descriptions were worded really well.

_____ Introduction was effective (attention getter, topic, and preview) at leading into the topic

_____ Body (Main Points) were clear and humorous

_____ Conclusion was effective at summarizing the topic, including a brief discussion of the social significance of the topic.

_____ Overall, the speech was really humorous. The speaker effectively included humorous examples.

Thanks for the courage to try this type of speech!

Motivational

Speaker:

Total time: (Note: 4-10 mins. with a 2 minute grace period)

Scale: 1-5 rating. (5 is the top A+ rating, 1 is the lowest rating)

_____ Overall, the speech exemplified your thorough understanding and application of things we have covered in class.

_____ Content: Overall the speech included effective examples.

_____ Organization: Good preview, summary, and transitions. The speech was easy to follow.

_____ Delivery: Good at using all those things from class: good eye contact, stance. Also good word use—descriptions were worded really well.

_____ Introduction was effective (attention getter, topic, and preview) at leading into the topic

_____ Body (Main Points) were clear and helped achieve the goal of motivating the audience

_____ Conclusion was effective at summarizing the topic, including a brief discussion of the social significance of the topic.

_____ Evidence: Good use of evidence. The citation was thorough and helped support your point.

_____ Overall, the speech was really motivational.

Commemorative

Speaker:

Total time: (Note: 4-10 mins. with a 2 minute grace period)

Scale: 1-5 rating. (5 is the top A+ rating, 1 is the lowest rating)

_____Overall, the speech exemplified your thorough understanding and application of things we have covered in class.

_____Content: Overall the speech included effective examples.

_____Organization: Good preview, summary, and transitions. The speech was easy to follow.

_____Delivery: Good at using all those things from class: good eye contact, stance. Also good word use—descriptions were worded really well.

_____Introduction was effective (attention getter, topic, and preview) at leading into the topic

_____Body (Main Points) were clear and helped achieve the goal of commemorating someone

_____Conclusion was effective at summarizing the topic, including a brief discussion of the social significance of the topic.

_____Evidence: Good use of testimonial evidence. The citation was thorough and helped support your point.

_____*Visual Aid use:* Good use of coordinating your visual aids into your speech. You described them well and they helped commemorate your subject.

_____Overall, the speech effectively paid tribute to someone.

Other: As Arranged with Instructor

Speaker:

Total time: (Note: 4-10 mins. with a 2 minute grace period)

Scale: 1-5 rating. (5 is the top A+ rating, 1 is the lowest rating)

_____Overall, the speech exemplified your thorough understanding and application of things we have covered in class.

_____Content: Overall the speech included effective examples.

_____Organization: Good preview, summary, and transitions. The speech was easy to follow.

_____Delivery: Good at using all those things from class: good eye contact, stance. Also good word use—descriptions were worded really well.

_____Introduction was effective (attention getter, topic, and preview) at leading into the topic

_____Body (Main Points) were clear and helped achieve the overall goal

_____Conclusion was effective at summarizing the topic, and wrapping up the speech with the reference back to the attention getter.

_____Evidence: Good use of testimonial or published evidence.

_____*Visual Aid use:* Good use of coordinating your visual aids into your speech. You described them well and they helped commemorate your subject.

_____Overall, the speech effectively achieved its goal.

Chapter 10: Humor in Speech

Humor can increase your credibility and gain the attention of the audience. Humor can also back fire if not used well. Try to work in a moderate amount of humor into your speech to start, as you develop more command with language and yourself as a speaker, incorporate more humor.

When to use humor

This depends on you and the situation

> At the beginning of your speech is a good place to include humor

> a) Note: don't over do it, especially if you are experimenting with humor in your speech

> b) Sometimes throughout the speech

Test your humor *PRIOR* to the speech

It's very difficult to see if your humor is really humorous, try it out on an audience or person prior.

How to use humor

It's best to select clean and appropriate humor—consider the audience here the humor first

Avoid targeting your humor to an out-group

Three Theories of Humor

1. **Incongruity theory:** breaking a pattern

2. **Superiority Theory:** making the audience feel superior

3. **Relief theory** (Freud's theory of humor): Audience laughs because anxiety is dispelled

Speech Analysis Paper – Part 1
An Analysis of My Public Speaking Expertise

The Speech Analysis Paper is a typed paper (single spaced) where you research, investigate, and analyze public speaking. Use the underlined headings provided. An additional area may be included, if so, it will be announced to the entire class at least a week prior to the due date. The analysis paper is evaluated based on completion, format, and analysis. Include a cover page—even a picture if you like and a table of contents of the below areas and your name and class meeting time. Submit the portfolio by stapling on the top left corner. Use APA or MLA format recommended.

1. <u>My Public Speaking Experiences:</u> Briefly describe and assess your speeches that you have done prior to this course. For each speech prior to class discussion should not exceed 150 words. Briefly describe and assess your class speeches to this point in the term (no word limit). This assessment should be based on your own self-assessment, the instructor's feedback, and; if applicable, feedback from your classmates. For each of the class speeches you have completed to this point. List all your speeches to this point and include at least three specific positives you achieved for each speech, and include at least one specific area to fix for each speech. Write the answer in list form or outline form. Include the grade feedback and student feedback.

2. <u>My Ideal Speech Process</u> What is your ideal speech creating process prior to delivering the actual speech? In other words, what specific things do you do to best create a speech from the very beginning until the point of delivery. Discuss this by giving a detailed step by step process. Write answers in bullet pointed list form or outline form.

3. <u>My Speech Anxiety:</u> Take the James McCroskey Communications Anxiety questionnaire http://www.wadsworth.com/communication_d/templates/student_resources/053456223X_ha milton/survey/prca/main_frame.htm. Please print the results (note: you can email the results to yourself and print out. What areas do you have the highest anxiety? What areas do you have the lowest anxiety? What are at least two things you will incorporate to manage your anxiety in future speeches?

4. <u>Speaking to Instruct.</u> Think of all the teachers you have ever had. Who was the most engaging teacher and why? Discuss the instructor's level of credibility: Link your discussion to the three credibility areas of: expertise, like-ability, and believe-ability? For each of these three areas, discuss how the instructor met the credibility area. Overall, what do you think makes an instructor's speaking effective?

5. <u>Speech and the Engineering Field</u>. Based on the study in <u>Communication Education</u> (July 2002) by Deanna Dannels p. 254, five important features of speaking in engineering were identified. What are these features? Give a brief definition of each and an example of each. Based on this article what does translation mean? Source: Dannels, D. (2002). Communication across the curriculum and in the disciplines: Speaking in engineering, *Communication Education, 51(3)*. p 254

Speech Analysis Paper – Part 2

The Speech Analysis Paper is a typed single spaced paper where you research, investigate, and analyze public speaking. Use the underlined headings provided. Organize each section of the paper in outline format (i.e., include sub-subheadings where needed). Include your paragraph based discussion within the outline frame. Include a cover page with at table of contents, your name, class meeting time, and optionally a picture. Submit the Speech Analysis Paper by stapling on the top left corner. The Speech Analysis Paper is evaluated based on completion, format, and analysis.

1. <u>My Public Speaking Experiences:</u> Briefly describe and assess your class speeches **to this point in the term** (no word limit). This assessment should be based on your own self-assessment, the instructor's feedback, and; if applicable, feedback from your classmates. List each individual speech that you have completed, for each speech identify at least three specific positives you have achieved for that particular speech, and include at least one specific area to fix for that speech. Write the answer in outline format. Include quotations for instructor and student feedback, and put the source of the feedback in parenthesis, for instance: The tone of the speech captured the overall goal of the speech (instructor).

2. <u>Visually Enhanced Speeches:</u> Think of the computer enhanced presentations (e.g., PowerPoint, Prezi, etc.) that you have seen. Discuss the most favorable one's and why. Discuss the most unfavorable ones and why? List your top 3-5 recommendations for effective computer enhanced presentations (PowerPoint). Locate, read and analyze the April 27, 2010 New York Times article, "We have met the enemy and he is PowerPoint." Your analysis should include a description of the key positions in the article. Additionally, include a description and analysis of: (1) what McMaster is referring to when he says PowerPoint is dangerous, and (2) what commanders say it [PowerPoint] stifles, and (3) your overall perspective on whether the same concerns from the article can be made outside of military environments (i.e., in Business, Healthcare, etc.).

3. <u>Group Discussion analysis</u> Analyze a group discussion that you participated in for your in-class team speech. If you did not do an in-class team/group speech, use a group discussion you participated in outside of this class. Analysis should include (1) *task accomplishment:* was the group able to achieve the tasks it set out to complete? If so, which ones? And how effective were the members at achieving key tasks? (2) *participation*: did everyone get to participate, or did the group rely on only a limited number of group members? Did everyone get along socially? Why so? Or why not? (3) *evidence of agreement*: what issues did your group members agree upon and how do you know (i.e., meeting notes/end of meeting review). (4) What would you want to see from the group members to improve the communication process and the final outcome (speech)?

4. <u>Speaking to coach/train:</u> Think back to an excellent former or current speaker (coach, trainer, etc.) who was trying to teach you how to do physically do something (something that requires some action and movement), such as teach you a certain dance routine, coach you on a sport, or how to cook something, fix something, and so forth. Answer these questions: (1) what techniques for explaining the activity were used and were these techniques effective? (2) If you were to coach or train an audience on how to do something, what would you teach about, and how specifically would you instruct the listener (give step-by-step sequence)?

5. <u>Martin Luther King Jr.'s "I Have a Dream" speech:</u> Analyze King's use of metaphor, repetition, alliteration/rhyming, and word-use in the speech. Refer to specific language in the speech in the discussion. What is your overall analysis of the speech and why?

6. <u>Beginning to end of the semester speech analysis:</u> Describe your public speaking ability from day one until now. At the beginning of class: what were your feelings, skills, knowledge, and anxiety about your public speaking ability. What are your current feelings, skills, knowledge, and anxiety as of this point? What areas do you believe you've significantly improved on and what public speaking areas to you want to work on in the future? Complete the PSDS Part 2. Include the summation page were you subtract PSDS Part 2 scores from Part 1 scores (last page of the survey).

Public Speaking Development Survey – Part 2
Self-Assessment Survey: PART 2

Competence Survey: this survey examines your level of speech anxiety, speech preparation ability, outline, deliver, and include evidence, compelling reasoning, and stories; visual aids coordination, and listening, and overall public speaking ability. Answer based on your own assessment of your speaking abilities. For each question, circle only one answer.

A. Excitement has to do with the positive emotional anticipation of doing a speech. It is the anticipation of something really positive that is about to occur. How much excitement do you have when you are about to deliver a speech?

1. None

2. Below average

3. Average

4. Above average

5. A high amount

B. If you decided to do a speech in two weeks, how would you prepare for the speech?

1. I would avoid preparing, since I'm good at just speaking off the cuff.

2. I would start by thinking of my speech, although it's unlikely I would have time to write it or outline it, I do like to mentally know what I'm going to say.

3. I would start by writing my speech out, starting with the beginning and going all the way to the end. After everything is written out, I would practice by reading it aloud.

4. I would prepare a lot. My preparation would include speaking and writing. I would start by creating my main points, by saying them and even outlining them. I would think of specific stories and good well-reasoned points. I would also do thorough research; then I would revise and refine the speech. I would then go through my introduction and conclusion in the same manner.

C. Outlining a speech has to do with the ability to highlight the main points of a given speech. This involves grouping the speech into sections, such as the Introduction, Body, and Conclusion. It also involves a visual representation of the speech through enumerations (lettering and numbering the points of a speech). How well can you put an outline together?

1. Not well at all

2. Below average

3. About average

4. Above average

5. I do excellent outlines

D. When presenting a speech, it is often necessary to divide up the speech into various areas/sections in the speech. When you deliver the speech are you able to create distinctive sections with your voice tone and even the wording, such as using transition sentences that help the audience understand clearly the introductory points you are making, each of the main body points you are making, and your concluding remarks?

1. No, this would be very difficult
2. Yes, but I would struggle to accomplish this
3. Yes, I can do this
4. Yes, I'm excellent at this

E. Delivery has to do with your oral presentation of the speech. It involves speaking with eye contact and the effective use of you voice and even body. How well can you deliver a speech?

1. Far below average
2. Below average
3. Average
4. Above average
5. I have excellent delivery

F. When delivering a speech, are you able to state the source (i.e., name of the magazine, date, authors and their credibility, and the basic connection) of your information completely and in less than 45 seconds?

1. No, this would be very difficult
2. Yes, but I would struggle to completely and clearly cite the information in that time-frame
3. Yes, I can do this
4. Yes, I'm excellent at this

G. When delivering a speech, are you able to include specific stories that relate to the point you are making?

1. No, this would be very difficult
2. Yes, but I would struggle to give a clear and timely story
3. Yes, I can do this
4. Yes, I'm excellent at this

H. If you were delivering a persuasive speech where you were attempting to persuade an audience by using good reasoning to support your points, would you be able to do this well?

1. No, this would be very difficult
2. Yes, but this would be very difficult
3. Yes, I can do this
4. Yes, I'm excellent at this

I. If you were to do a speech with visual aids, such as a PowerPoint speech; are you effective at including visual aids?

> 1. No, this would be very difficult
>
> 2. Yes, but this would be very difficult
>
> 3. Yes, I can do this
>
> 4. Yes, I'm excellent at this

J. As a listener of Public Speaking, can you make good distinctions between opinion and fact, key issues and minor issues, good reasoning and evidence versus poor or biased reasoning and evidence?

> 1. No, this would be very difficult
>
> 2. Yes, but this would be very difficult
>
> 3. Yes, I can do this
>
> 4. Yes, I'm excellent at this

K. Can you design and deliver an effective speech?

> 1. No, this would be very difficult
>
> 2. Yes, but this would be very difficult
>
> 3. Yes, I can do this
>
> 4. Yes, I'm excellent at this

PSDS SCORING:

	Part 2 Score	Part 1 Score	Subtract Part 2 score from Part 1 Score
Sample Scoring			
Question A =	3	1	3 – 1 = +2
Question B =	2	4	2 – 4 = -2

This is your improvement from the beginning of the semester to the end of the semester.

	Part 2 Score	Part 1 Score	Subtract Part 2 score from Part 1 Score
			[This is your improvement from the beginning to the end of the semester]
Question A = [Anxiety]	___	___	___
Question B = [Speech Preparation]	___	___	___
Question C = [Outlining]	___	___	___
Question D = [Organizing]	___	___	___
Question E = [Delivery]	___	___	___
Question F = [Evidence]	___	___	___
Question G = [Narrative Stories]	___	___	___
Question H = [Persuasiveness]	___	___	___
Question I = [Visual Aid Use]	___	___	___
Question J = [Listening]	___	___	___
Question H = [Overall Speech Effectiveness]	___	___	___

What is the total score of the last column (Improvement Column) =

Criteria for 10-Minute Formal Speech
Public Speaking Criteria for a formal platform speech of 10 minutes

I. **APPROACH TO SPEAKING AREA:** From the time you are introduced to the time you actually start speaking

A. Continuity to the speaking stage
A smooth confident walk up to the speaking stage (front of class).

B. Appearance
In general, you should dress profession/business attire/more formal. Try dressing as if you are going on an important interview. Also, avoid clothing and hair style that will block eye contact. No hats, no sun glasses, and avoid your hair draping over your face. Make a mindful consciences decision for yourself what would be the most appropriate.

C. Pause/establish eye contact
Prior to speaking, pause and span your audience to make sure the audience is ready.

II. **INTRODUCTION:** Approximately the first 10-20% of your speech, where the speaker introduces the speech.

A. Attention Getter (A must!)
The very first part of a speech where the speaker gets the audiences interest in the speech. Examples: activity, story, quotation, statistic, audience question & answer, and more. Your attention getter:
a) should be creative
b) should relate to the topic

B. Purpose statement
The part just after the attention getter where the speaker reveals the theme or general topic of the speech. Sometimes (such as in a controversial persuasive) the purpose in not revealed early. In general, a purpose statement:
a) Is one to two sentences only. Short!
b) Doesn't reveal too much here; you will get to discuss in-depth later

C. Preview (A must!): The part after the purpose statement, where the speaker explicitly identifies the key areas he or she will discuss.
a) about 1 sentence
b) *For the beginner,* make the preview very specific (for example "Today, I want to discuss, first: the history of Rio Hondo College; second, interesting academic programs at Rio Hondo, upcoming Rio Hondo developments
c) *For more advanced speakers,* craft the preview in a more rhetorical way ("...we'll look at Rio Hondo's historical origins, its education programs, and finally the future developments at this higher education institution.")

D. Credibility established: One or two sentences where the speaker establishes trustworthiness or competence. Usually citing an early source, or highlighting a speaker's direct connection with the topic. Can be integrated into attention getter or purpose statement. I suggest, if not integrated, to put between attention getter and purpose statement

E. <u>Rationale:</u> A short section where the speaker tells the audience why they should listen to the speech. Describing how does the topic directly affect the audience members.

F. <u>Premised a sensitive topic</u> [sometimes necessary]: A short section where the speaker cushions the audience about the sensitive nature of his/her speech.

III. BODY (structure): how the body is structured

<u>Rationale for organized body:</u>
1. Audience will understand the speech better
2. Audience will judge the speaker of an organized speech as more competent & trustworthy (credibility)

<u>Main Points</u>
1. For a 5-10 minute speech 2-5 main points only
   A. using only 2 points = a speaker can discuss each point more in-depth
   B. using 3 points = a good average; recommended
   C. using 4,5 points = ok, but possible information overload. Hit points quickly.

2. Organize based on similar areas. For example, if your points are the past, present, and future of Rio Hondo College; when discussing the past—only use info. that refers to Rio Hondo's past.

3. Each main point should be distinctive

4. Try to use similar wording, phrases, or sentences to identify the main point. In the topic below, for example, the word developments would help cue the audience that you are transitioning to another area.
   Central Theme: Reintroduction of wolves
   Specific Purpose: To inform the audience about the reintroduction efforts of the wolf in the U.S.
   (1) Developments during the 1980's
   (2) Developments during 1990's
   (3) Recent developments: 2000

5. Balance your time on each main point

BODY (content): what is said (the stories, examples, statistics, etc. used)

1. *Main points were understandable*
2. *Main points were insightful*
3. *Statistical Evidence integrated well*
4. *Narrative Evidence integrated well*
5. *Sufficient examples and support used*
6. *Critical questions were addressed*

IV. CONCLUSION

1. **Transition to conclusion:** *Although a speaker can simply indicate this verbally, "So in conclusion,"*

2. **Concluding summary:** *The speaker should summarize his/her main points ("so, today I have discussed....). Try making the summary to the point. The summary also will function as a transitional sentence to the conclusion.*

3. **Unified speech with the attention getter:** *Return to the introductory story of the speech*

LANGUAGE USE

Word choice: Use words, phrases, sentences, metaphors, analogies that clarify and help in the understanding of your speech.

Limited colloquialisms: Avoid cuss words and slang jargon, these deter from the content and decrease a speaker's credibility.

Limit vocal pauses: Avoid using "ahs" "like" "ums" and so forth as fillers—these vocal pauses make the speaker seem unsure of him/herself and diminish the speaker's credibility and speeches understandability. Just pause.

Defined or explained terms not known by audience: Briefly define or explain the meanings of terms that may not be known by the audience.

DELIVERY

Eye contact: The speaker should try to make direct eye contact with the audience. The speaker should try to really connect with the audience.

Eye span: The speaker should span the entire audience during the speech. The speaker should divide up the audience into sections and make eye contact with each of those sections over the course of his/her speech.

Stance: The speaker should stand in a way that is not distracting. In general the speaker should stand symmetric and confident.

Gestures: Gesticulate naturally, but don't over-do it. Your hands should be relaxed at your side, then gesticulate when needed.

Movement: Either stay in one place throughout the speech or coordinate your movement with the triangle movement. If coordinating movement, use the move-plant-deliver method. The speaker should coordinate movement with transitional phrases. Keep your eyes on the audience and continue speaking as you move.

Pace/vocal variety: This speaker's delivery pace should be varied and interesting. Try starting at a slow yet intense pace, and progressing to a slightly faster pace. Then, at the conclusion dropping your pace and inflection to a slow pace again. Drop inflection and pace for transitions.

Projection: Your vocal projection should be loud enough for everyone to hear you.

Pauses: The use of silence and pauses is one of the most powerful tools a speaker can use. Pause and use silence at selective times in your speech. Avoid vocal pauses.

Use of note cards: The speaker, when using note cards, should use them as memory aids only. Do not read too much from note cards. Keep your focus on the audience occasionally looking at note cards. Use index note cards (5 x 7 inch or smaller). Do not fidget with note cards. Do not allow note cards to distract the audience's focus.

Visual Aids: Effective use of high grade visual aids is required. Plan and coordinate the physical management of your visual aids. Adhere to the 10 suggestions for Visual Aid effectiveness in the book.

Speech Aids/Objects: If used plan and coordinate the use of these in manner where you direct the audience's focus, and enhance the speech through the use of these aids and objects.

ORGANIZATION

Easy to follow speech: The speaker should always make the speech easy to follow. Do things that enable the audience to follow the speech. For example, give narrative examples and real cases that enable the audience to absorb the main points. Organize the speech in a logical easy to understand manner. Deliver the speech in a way that enables all audience members to easily follow along.

Transitions: The speaker should use strong transitions. Use previews and signposts within your speech for transitions. Transitions should be verbal and nonverbal. *Verbally* you should say it: i.e. "now that I have discussed the problems with changing current bilingual education standards, let me now turn to the solutions." *Nonverbally* try saying the same sentence, but this time deliberately slow the pace and inflection of the underlined section: "now that I have discussed the problems with changing current bilingual education standards; <u>let me now turn to the solutions.</u>") Experiment using pauses and inflection changes to see the emphasis on each area.

Good balance of time on points: If you have four main points, allocate a general balance of time on each of those points.

GENERAL COMMUNICATIVE EFFECT

Topic choice: Pick a topic that is appropriate to the type of speech you are doing. Narrow the topic to meet the time frame. For instance, the topic "Music" is too broad. The topic "To inform my audience about salsa music" is better. I suggest you review newspapers, magazines, and your own interests to choose the best topic for both you and your audience.

Creativity: The speaker should add creative aspects in the speech.

Poise: If there is a distraction, keep your poise and this will benefit your speech.

Energy: Speak with a good level of intensity for your topic. If you communicate care for your topic, many the audience will reciprocate your interest in that topic.

Humor: The speaker should occasionally use humor in the speech. As long as the humor is not over done or too risqué (shocking), humor is a good way to personalize a speech. Try pausing for audience laughter when using humor.

Emotional balance/ build up: The speaker should try to evoke varied audience emotions throughout the speech. Like a good movie—there should be a little bit of everything. For instance, at times the speech should be very matter of fact, perhaps with statistics; other times, the speech should be more intense, perhaps with a dramatic story of the amazing thing that happened to one person.

Unveiling of the story: When telling a story the speaker should effectively tell the story. Try describing the situation or leading the audience through the story by giving each distinctive detailed story through the story.

Audience participation: This has to do with the speaker asking audience questions. Try starting with closed ended questions, open ended questions are fine but be aware of the constraints (time, speaker response, etc.)

Criteria for an Engineering Design Speech

In her analysis of speech criteria in the field of engineering, Deanna Dannels (2002) found that there were several criteria that an engineer should employ in the presentation. Engineers have a technical specialty that requires them to often communicate with audience members who do not have that specialty. Dannels' findings reveal the following criteria for presentations done by engineers:

1. **<u>Effective presentations should be simple</u>**

   Your audience is not all technically proficient in the area you are presenting about, so the presenter will need to translate technical information into a form that is simple and clear for lay audiences.

   To reach the audience, the presenter may need to speak the audience's language and use simple terms.

2. **<u>Effective presentations sell an idea:</u>**

   Presentations should persuade the audience to buy the idea/product. The audience should be persuaded to buy into the product you're trying to sell.

3. **<u>Effective presentations are numerically rich</u>**

   Include numerical evidence in your presentation such as statistics to prove your point.

4. **<u>Effective presentations are results oriented</u>**

   What are the results of your presentation. If the presenter was investigating something, the audience will want to know the results of what was found.

5. **<u>Effective presentations are visually sophisticated</u>**

   Use a visual image to represent your idea.

From Dannels, D. P. (2002). Communication Across the Curriculum and in the Disciplines: Speaking in engineering. *Communication Education (51),* p254-268.